Fantastic Families

Fantastic Families

W O R K B O O K

SHAPING THE FUTURE

J OE B EAM AND
D R . N ICK S TINNETT

HOWARD BOOKS
A DIVISION OF SIMON & SCHUSTER
New York   London   Toronto   Sydney
®

Our purpose at Howard Books is to:

- *Increase faith* in the hearts of growing Christians

- *Inspire holiness* in the lives of believers

- *Instill hope* in the hearts of struggling people everywhere

Because He's coming again!

Published by Howard Books, a division of Simon & Schuster, Inc.
1230 Avenue of the Americas, New York, NY 10020
www.howardpublishing.com

Fantastic Families Workbook © 2000 by Joe Beam and Dr. Nick Stinnett

Library of Congress Cataloging-in-Publication Data
Stinnett, Nick.
    Fantastic Families workbook : shaping the future / Joe Beam, Nick Stinnett.
        p. cm.
    Includes bibliographical references.
    ISBN-13: 978-1-58229-144-4

    1. Family—United States—Handbooks, manuals, etc. 2. Family—Religious aspects—Christianity. I. Beam, Joe. II. Title.

    HQ535 .S74 2000
    306.85'0973—dc21   00-031980

10 9 8 7 6 5 4 3 2

HOWARD colophon is a registered trademark of Simon & Schuster, Inc.

Manufactured in United States of America

For information regarding special discounts for bulk purchases, please contact: Simon & Schuster Special Sales at 1-800-456-6798 or business@simonandschuster.com.

Edited by Stephanie Terry
Interior Design by Kathryn Murray
Photography by Lamar

Publisher's Note: Because everyone's particular situation is unique, the ideas and suggestions contained in this book should not be considered a substitute for consultation with a psychiatrist or trained therapist.

Scripture quotations are from the *Holy Bible, New International Version.* Copyright © 1973, 1978, 1984 International Bible Society. Used by permission of Zondervan.

◆ CONTENTS ◆

SOME THINGS YOU NEED TO KNOW

This workbook will help all families, whether they use it on their own or, for the absolute best results, as participants in Family Dynamics Institute's eight-week interactive course called *Fantastic Families*. We encourage you to provide an individual workbook for each parent and for every child who can read and write. That way each person can be honest in how he or she answers questions, not fearing censure, rejection, or ridicule.

In addition to the *Fantastic Families* book and *Fantastic Families: Shaping the Future Workbook,* those enrolled in the course will receive additional materials such as a student handbook and a series of audio cassettes. Several families—traditional families, single-parent families, blended families—meet together once each week for eight weeks in a two-and-a-half-hour session that is fun, fast-paced, and life-changing. Children age 13 and up also attend the seminar sessions. Children under that age participate in the weekly family sessions at home. This powerful course is scientifically designed to deepen relationships between all family members, even those who may have poor relationships now. Specially trained and certified facilitators lead the *Fantastic Families* course. For information on how to enroll your family in this eight-week interactive course, or to get more information on how to become a certified facilitator, call 1-800-650-9995, or visit www.familydynamics.net. To speak with someone, call 1-706-855-9900.

WHAT MAKES A FAMILY
STRONG, HEALTHY, AND HAPPY?

Welcome to eight weeks of fun family exercises and activities!

It will be more fun than not, but we have to alert you to one aspect of this workbook before you begin. Mixed in with the pleasurable may be an exercise or two that will make some members of the family uncomfortable. We'd like it if all growth came easily and no unpleasant subjects had to be broached, but real life isn't that way. Whether we like it or not, "no *pain*, no *gain*" is one of those proverbs that contains more truth than myth.

Gain. An interesting word. Webster's gives it definitions like "to get (something desired)...to obtain as a profit...to win...to reach...to improve; make progress; advance."[1]

That's why you purchased this workbook, isn't it? You want your family to profit, win, improve, and advance. You want every member of your family to be stronger, better equipped to face the world. You want to be extremely effective in preparing your children to make worthwhile lives of their own. While achieving those goals, you want to make your home as happy and safe as it can possibly be. You want God to be in, around, and throughout your family.

Are we right? Is that what you crave; what you seek?

Good news. That's what this workbook offers.

As you've seen in *Fantastic Families*, the accompanying book on which this workbook is based, we intend to show you how to implement for your family the six powerful secrets for family success. Drs. Nick Stinnett and John DeFrain validated these six characteristics of strong families through more than twenty-five years of research with families in all fifty states and twenty-four countries around the world. At last count about forty master's theses and doctoral dissertations have been written on these six principles. When a family uses all six of these principles, it becomes strong and stays strong. To the degree a family doesn't implement one or more of the principles, it becomes correspondingly weaker.

Understanding the universal effectiveness of these six principles, you'll want to make the effort and do the work to ground your family in every one of these principles.

They work.

If you've enrolled in Family Dynamics's interactive *Fantastic Families* course, your entire family will experience an extraordinary eight weeks. Not only will you learn from the book, workbook, and each family member over the next eight weeks, you'll also gain revealing insights from your specially trained and certified facilitator and the other families in your course. We've designed this interactive course to do more for you than teach good information: It will change the way you relate with each other. Because of our experience with thousands of families who have participated in FDI interactive seminars around the world, we confidently anticipate your family's bonding more deeply than you ever could have imagined as you complete each course session.

THE SIX CHARACTERISTICS OF STRONG FAMILIES

What are the universal characteristics of strong families?

1. *Commitment*. Members of strong families are dedicated to promoting each other's welfare and happiness. They value the unity of the family.

2. *Appreciation and Affection*. Members of strong families show appreciation for each other a great deal. They can feel how good a family is.

3. *Positive Communication*. Members of good families have good communication skills and spend large amounts of time talking with each other.

4. *Time Together*. Strong families spend time—quality time in generous quantities—with each other.

5. *Spiritual Well-Being*. Whether they go to formal religious services or not, strong families have a sense of a greater good or power in life. That belief gives them strength and purpose.

6. *The Ability to Cope with Stress and Crises*. Members of strong families are able to view stress or crises as opportunities to grow.

In this chapter we give you an exercise to determine how your family rates each of these characteristics. In the following chapters we lead you through exercises to increase the presence of each characteristic in your family life.

Before we get started, we need to emphasize three guidelines to follow as you work through this study.

GUIDELINES

Complete one chapter each week. If you follow that schedule, in just eight short weeks you'll have advanced through this entire workbook, including the exercises in this introduction. Why stay with so strict a regimen? Because some of these exercises will really make you think, and some of them will lead to sessions of unmasked sharing with each other. That can be emotionally draining at times, just as it can be emotionally exhilarating at others. If you take too long or don't follow a specific schedule, you'll never finish. Therefore, to gain the most from the exercises, make yourselves stay on schedule. If you're in the *Fantastic Families* interactive course, the facilitators and other class members will help you stay motivated and on track.

Don't skip any exercises or chapters. Take things in order. Even when the reason for the order isn't apparent to you, be assured that we designed these exercises to flow from one to the other. If you skip one, you may discover a few exercises down the line that ask you to incorporate information you wrote in a previous exercise. Obviously, if you've skipped that called-for exercise, you won't be able to complete the one that you're currently working on. So please stay on track and stay in order.

Always write down your answers to the questions. (Of course, this applies only to family members who can write!) It isn't good enough just to tell your spouse or your children what your answer is. Good teachers and trainers understand this basic truth: You can talk without thinking, but you cannot write without thinking. The very act of writing your answer will take you to deeper levels of understanding of yourself, your spouse, your children, your parent(s), and the principles for developing a stronger, happier family. We've even provided an extra-wide margin for taking notes as you think and work through the exercises.

In some chapters you'll notice that the exercises call for you to answer questions that are similar to questions you answered in earlier chapters. Don't despair; that's by design. We know from our work with families that you will evolve in your view of these questions as you work through the chapters. As you grow in understanding each other, you should be sharing that growth and those evolving thoughts. The occasional repetitive nature of questions about specific, important family matters not only allows but also creates the right scenario for you to share your personal growth—whether gradual or rapid.

Follow these guidelines and in eight weeks you will have more peace, harmony, and love in your family.

The exercises in this chapter will take time to finish. If you have children under twelve or children not yet ready to understand and participate in the exercises, we suggest that the parent(s) and older, more mature children complete exercise 1 together before involving the rest of the family in the other two exercises. If there is only one parent and no older children, then the parent should complete the first exercise alone. Of course, families with older children may not need to complete exercise 1 at all. Read it and decide whether it applies to your family.

We designed the exercises in this chapter to bring family members closer together. Be aware that as you incorporate younger family members into these exercises, they may react with resentment if the sessions are too long. Therefore, we recommend that you set a maximum time limit (appropriate for your family members' ages and temperaments) for each session. It's better to have two sessions or to slightly speed up a project to finish in a prescribed time limit than to turn these exercises into dreaded drudgery. Have fun! If everyone is enjoying themselves, let a session run longer. Remember, these exercises are made for your family, not your family for these exercises.

We strongly urge you to plan a meeting of the entire family during the week to complete exercises 2 and 3. As you plan your meeting, please remember the extremely important advice in the following text box.

Each person may read ahead and jot down responses to each of the exercises. Those helping younger children should make notes on their responses so they can help them during the sharing time included in the family meeting. During the family meetings, everyone will share what he or she has written.

EXERCISE 1: UNDERSTANDING EACH PERSON'S ROLE

◆ ◆ ◆

Any family—no matter what the combination of people—can make effective use of this workbook. Maybe you're a single parent with one or more children. Or it could be that you're a couple without children. It's even possible that you're a large family unit that includes more than parents and children: Grandparents, aunts, uncles, or cousins also are an integral part of your daily family life. That's okay. Whatever the composition of your family, this workbook is for you.

We said above that even very young children may participate and learn. In every chapter we'll give you guidance on how family members in every age group can use the principles in that chapter to make your family stronger. On pages 211–212 in Appendix C of the *Fantastic Families* book, we tell of the work of Virginia Bert and Kathleen Funderburk. They developed the Family/School/Community Partnership Program at the Florida State University School that educates kindergarten through grade 12. The six characteristics of strong families formed the foundation of their program model and were used in the family education programs, the school curriculum, and in guiding the supportive partnerships among the families, the school, and the community. On page 12 of the Executive Summary of Family/School/Community Partnership, A Model for Strengthening Families, they give the following chart. This chart will help you determine the level of involvement your children are capable of for the exercises each week.

| MATURATIONAL TASKS—BIRTH THROUGH ADOLESCENCE			
Age	**Physical/Cognitive Tasks**	**Age**	**Social/Emotional Tasks**
0–1	**Infancy**	0–1	**Infancy**
	Eye-hand coordination		Learning to eat solid foods
	Sensory discrimination		Achieving emotional stability
	Simple motor skills		
	No moral concepts		
1–2	**Toddlerhood**	1–2	**Toddlerhood**
	Walking/Talking		Controlling body elimination
	Increasing self-reliance and independence; autonomy		Adjusting to socialization demands
	Fear of punishment		Beginning social play
	Egocentric hedonism		
2–6	**Early Childhood**	2–6	**Early Childhood**
	Skill learning and general bodily control		Learning cultural rules and expectations
	Fine muscle control		Learning about sex roles
	Developing and refining concepts of social and physical reality; right and wrong		Relating emotionally to family members and, later, to others, such as relatives and peers
	Learning about sex differences developing an accurate body concept		
	Learning through exploration, manipulation play		
	Desire to please; adjusting to rules		

6–12	Middle Childhood	6–12	Middle Childhood
	Learning to learn through reading and other informative activities		Relating to teacher and other unfamiliar adults
	Learning basic facts of science, math, and humanities		Achieving independence within the family
	Distinguishing fact from fantasy		Meeting expectations of peers, reference groups
	Learning through hobbies and recreational activities		Developing conscience and self-regulation of behavior
	Coping with frustration		Coping with gender role expectations and other external pressures
	Upholding rules and laws		Developing frustration tolerance
12+	Adolescence	12+	Adolescence
	Mastering conceptual and theoretical aspects of science, math, and humanities		Adjusting to body changes, new emotions
	Learning about and being able to apply knowledge needed for adaptation in general and occupational choice		Achieving gradual independence from adults
	Mature sense of identity		Questioning values and reaffirming them or finding new ones
	Development of abstract moral philosophies based on ideas of rights; privileges		Achieving intimate personal relationships
			Ultimately choosing mate, vocation

In each chapter of this workbook, we include ideas from the Executive Summary to help you know how to involve each person in your family in developing that chapter's characteristic. Right now, we encourage you to examine carefully the above chart and answer these questions.

1. What ideas can you come up with to involve each family member on his or her level? (Remember that the above chart serves as a starting point for your ideas.)

We can involve _____ by _____

We can involve _____ by _____

We can involve _____ by _____

We can involve _____ by _____

We can involve _____ by _____

We can involve _____ by _____

2. Now, let each older family member take turns deciding how to specifically adapt each chapter's exercises for the younger members (or anyone who has difficulty reading or understanding). That adaptation depends more on your knowledge of family members than it does on the suggestions we provide. Use the following form to volunteer to work ahead and design applications for specific family members for specific chapters. (You may help more than one family member during a specified chapter.)

When it comes time to adapt the exercises for each chapter, you should first read all the exercises, then go to the end of that chapter (under the heading "Helping Others") to find a few ideas for involving every person in your family in these exercises.

- ◆ For chapter _____, I, _____, volunteer to work a week ahead and design a way for _____ to participate in the exercises and contribute to our family's growth.

- ◆ For chapter _____, I, _____, volunteer to work a week ahead and design a way for _____ to participate in the exercises and contribute to our family's growth.

◆ For chapter _____, I, _____, volunteer to work a week ahead and design a way for _____ to participate in the exercises and contribute to our family's growth.

◆ For chapter _____, I, _____, volunteer to work a week ahead and design a way for _____ to participate in the exercises and contribute to our family's growth.

◆ For chapter _____, I, _____, volunteer to work a week ahead and design a way for _____ to participate in the exercises and contribute to our family's growth.

◆ For chapter _____, I, _____, volunteer to work a week ahead and design a way for _____ to participate in the exercises and contribute to our family's growth.

◆ For chapter _____, I, _____, volunteer to work a week ahead and design a way for _____ to participate in the exercises and contribute to our family's growth.

◆ For chapter _____, I, _____, volunteer to work a week ahead and design a way for _____ to participate in the exercises and contribute to our family's growth.

3.   Bring the group together to discuss what each has written for numbers 1 and 2 above. When you come to a consensus, list here what each person will do to help plan/design activities and applications as you work through the remainder of this workbook.

EXERCISE 2:
DISCOVERING WHERE YOU ARE NOW

◆ ◆ ◆

In Appendix A of the *Fantastic Families* book, we give a tool for assessing family strengths. We reproduce that assessment tool here. Each family member capable of reading and understanding the statements should complete the assessment on his or her own. For those who either cannot read the statements or cannot yet comprehend every statement, another family member should read and explain the statements. When explaining a statement, be careful not to inadvertently change its meaning!

ASSESSING YOUR FAMILY'S STRENGTHS

Each family member should give his or her own answers for the questions below. (There is one exception: You will notice that statement 3 applies to husband and wife only.) Put an "S" for *strength* beside those qualities you feel your family has achieved, and a "G" for *growth* beside those qualities that are areas of potential growth. If the particular characteristic does not apply to your family or is not a characteristic important to you, put an "NA" for *not applicable*.

By doing this exercise, family members will be able to identify those areas they would like to work on together to improve and those areas of strength that will serve as the foundation for their growth and positive change together.

COMMITMENT

1. _____ We are "always there" for each other.

2. _____ We are dedicated to our marriage as the core of the family.

3. _____ We (spouses) are faithful to each other sexually.

4. _____ We value each family member as a precious part of the family.

5. _____ We take care of each other and help each other.

6. _____ We share many family goals.

7. _____ We give family priority over outside activities, including work.

8. _____ We are honest with each other.

9. _____ We have numerous family traditions.

10. _____ We will endure/stay together as a family.

11. _____ We have unconditional love for each other.

12. _____ We can depend on each other.

13. _____ We make sacrifices for our family.

14. _____ Give an overall rating (S or G) of *commitment* in your family.

APPRECIATION AND AFFECTION

15. _____ We show appreciation to each other every day.

16. _____ We feel deep and genuine affection for each other.

17. _____ We avoid criticizing each other.

18. _____ We speak positively to each other.

19. _____ We recognize each other's accomplishments.

20. _____ We see each other's good qualities.

21. _____ We look for the good in each other (dig for diamonds).

22. _____ We are sincere in our expressions of appreciation.

23. _____ We practice good manners at home and with others.

24. _____ We refrain from sarcasm and put-downs.

25. _____ We cultivate gentle, positive humor. (No one is embarrassed or hurt by it.)

26. _____ We accept compliments and kindnesses graciously.

27. _____ We create a pleasant environment at home.

28. _____ We enhance each other's self-esteem.

29. _____ We feel safe and secure in our interactions with each other.

30. _____ Give an overall rating (S or G) of *appreciation and affection* in your family.

POSITIVE COMMUNICATION

31. _____ We allow time for communication (conversations, discussions).

32. _____ We have positive communication.

33. _____ We listen to each other.

34. _____ We check the meaning of messages (give feedback, seek clarification).

35. _____ We see things from each other's point of view (have empathy).

36. _____ We avoid criticizing, judging, or acting superior.

37. _____ We are honest and truthful (and kind).

38. _____ We deal with disagreements promptly.

39. _____ We deal with conflict issues one at a time.

40. _____ We are specific when dealing with conflict issues.

41. _____ We seek compromise or consensus in resolving conflict (rather than "win or lose").

42. _____ We avoid actions and words that would be emotionally devastating to each other.

43. _____ We seek to understand and accept our differences.

44. _____ Give an overall rating (S or G) of *positive communication* in your family.

TIME TOGETHER

45. _____ We eat meals together regularly.

46. _____ We do house and yard chores together.

47. _____ We spend time together in recreation (play).

48. _____ We participate in religious activities together.

49. _____ We attend school or social activities together.

50. _____ We celebrate holidays, birthdays, and anniversaries as a family.

51. _____ We have a family vacation.

52. _____ We enjoy each other's company.

53. _____ We have good times together that are unplanned and spontaneous.

54. _____ We take time to be with each other.

55. _____ We spend good quality time together.

56. _____ Give an overall rating (S or G) of *time together* in your family.

SPIRITUAL WELL-BEING

57. _____ We believe that God has a purpose for our lives.

58. _____ We have moral beliefs and values that guide us (honesty, responsibility).

59. _____ We practice virtues such as patience, forgiveness, and controlling anger.

60. _____ We have inner peace even in difficult times because of our relationship with God.

61. _____ We have an outlook on life that is usually hopeful and confident.

62. _____ We believe that God watches over and guides our family.

63. _____ We are part of a church family.

64. _____ We have family and friends who share our spiritual beliefs.

65. _____ We praise God for his love and involvement in our family.

66. _____ We attend worship services as a family.

67. _____ We read and study the Bible and other Christian literature.

68. _____ We spend time each day in prayer.

69. _____ We meditate on God's Word.

70. _____ We apply our spiritual values to everyday life.

71. _____ We avoid extreme or ongoing arguments over beliefs.

72. _____ Give an overall rating (S or G) of *spiritual well-being* in your family.

ABILITY TO COPE WITH STRESS AND CRISES

73. _____ We are able to ignore petty irritants and minor stresses.

74. _____ We don't give lots of attention or energy to worry.

75. _____ We believe that daily struggles/challenges are just a part of reaching a bigger goal.

76. _____ We use humor to relieve stress and tension.

77. _____ We take life one day at a time.

78. _____ We eliminate some involvements when our schedules get too full.

79. _____ We give attention/energy to the most important things first.

80. _____ We engage in recreational activities and hobbies.

81. _____ We enjoy outdoor relaxation and recreation.

82. _____ We participate in regular exercise.

83. _____ We manage to see some good in bad situations.

84. _____ We work together to face the challenges of crises.

85. _____ We support each other emotionally in crisis situations.

86. _____ We seek help from friends, church, and neighbors during crises.

87. _____ We seek professional help in crisis situations.

88. _____ We call on spiritual resources (God's help, faith, hope) in times of crises.

89. _____ We see opportunities for personal and family growth in crisis situations.

90. _____ We use good communication to share feelings and to solve problems.

91. _____ We are flexible and adaptable.

92. _____ Give an overall rating (S or G) of *ability to cope with stress and crises* in your family.

When everyone has completed the survey, it's time for the family to discuss it. Follow these ground rules for discussion:

- No one may be censured, criticized, or in any way made to feel bad because of the answers he or she gives.

- Everyone has permission to share what he or she really feels.
- Each person's feelings will be respected, even if he or she is the only person in the family to feel that way.

Now, elect a chairperson to lead the discussion (usually a parent considered by the majority to be fair and evenhanded). The chairperson designates a secretary to record the number of "S," "G," and "NA" assessments given to each statement. The chairperson starts with the family member sitting on his or her right and goes around the room one person at a time getting each person's assessment.

Once all assessments are tallied, the chairperson again starts with the person on his or her right and asks why each person gave the assessment he or she did. Take your time and let each person explain as much as he or she likes. Other family members may ask questions for clarification, but if anyone in any way indicates displeasure or disagreement, the chairperson must intervene. Openness and honesty must be established in this meeting, or subsequent meetings will suffer. It is much more important to have family members share their real feelings than to try to force everyone to see things the same way.

When the discussion is finished, the entire family examines the tally sheet and decides which characteristic is the strongest in their family and which is the weakest.

Write the strongest characteristic in your family here.

Write the weakest characteristic in your family here.

The chairperson collects the tally sheet and files it for use in the last chapter of this workbook.

Putting It to Work—Six Ideas for Your Family

Now that your family has an idea of where it currently is in terms of the six characteristics, it's time to set goals as to where you want to be in eight weeks.

1. The chairperson asks every person to take from five to ten minutes to list three specific goals they would like for the family to accomplish that would overcome the weakest characteristic. The goals may be generic ("let's be closer") or more specific ("let's have a family outing once a month").

2. When everyone is finished, the chairperson starts with the family member on his or her left and has each person share one goal. The secretary records the

goals. As each goal is shared, others may ask clarification questions, but no one may indicate any negative attitude about the goal in any way. The chairperson must intervene if anyone does.

3. After the first round, two more rounds take place in the same manner.

4. When finished, the secretary reads all the goals slowly so that everyone is reminded of what each goal is.

5. After the reading, the chairperson calls for a vote to determine the three goals that the family will work on.

6. Once the three goals are established, the family discusses each one in detail. Each goal must be honed to answer the following questions.

   ◆ How can we make this goal specific enough so that we will know when we actually accomplish it? (For example, how would you know you had become "closer"? What criteria would let you know that you had become closer?)

   ◆ What date will the family agree on for completing this goal?

   ◆ How could the family measure the incremental accomplishment of this goal? (For example, if you intend to have a goal accomplished within eight weeks, how can you measure how much of the goal you've achieved during each of the intervening seven weeks?)

When the family agrees on the three goals and those goals have been honed to meet the above criteria, write the three goals here.

Specific family goal number 1:

We will accomplish this goal by this date: _____.
The way we will measure it in the meantime is

Specific family goal number 2:

We will accomplish this goal by this date: _____.
The way we will measure it in the meantime is

Specific family goal number 3:

We will accomplish this goal by this date: _____.
The way we will measure it in the meantime is

Congratulations on a good start into the *Fantastic Families: Shaping the Future Workbook*. The next seven weeks will be wonderful!

STEP ONE
COMMIT TO
YOUR FAMILY

Remember what Jesus had to say about foundations?

> A wise man...built his house on the rock. The rain came down, the streams rose, and the winds blew and beat against that house; yet it did not fall, because it had its foundation on the rock.... A foolish man...built his house on sand. The rain came down, the streams rose, and the winds blew and beat against that house, and it fell with a great crash.[1]

When it comes to building a strong family, think of commitment as the foundation. The solid foundation. The foundation crucial to the support of everyone in the family and everything needed by the family.

Think of commitment as the bedrock of love.

In his book about developing intimacy in marriage, *Becoming ONE*,[2] Joe Beam described the spiritual aspects of the dimensions of love delineated in research by Dr. Robert Sternberg of Yale University. Sternberg clearly demonstrates that love has three dimensions—commitment, intimacy, and passion. When all three exist in a marriage relationship, they create a beautiful ONEness between husband and wife.

They also create a wonderful oneness within a family.

While the role of passion in a family obviously differs dramatically from that in a husband/wife relationship, each of the three dimensions affects the way each family member loves other family members. Commitment forms the rock-solid foundation, binding them together. Intimacy creates feelings of warmth, closeness, and acceptance. Passion drives the desire to be with each other and to protect each other from any harm. Without taking space here to discuss again what has already been written in *Becoming ONE*, allow us to briefly show how each of the six characteristics of strong families blends perfectly with Sternberg's dimensions of love.

Six Characteristics	Sternberg's Love Components
Commitment	Commitment (I will be here for you.)
Appreciation and Affection Positive Communication Spend Time Together	Intimacy (I understand you and like you.)
Spiritual Well-Being Cope with Stress and Crises	Passion (We are part of each other.)

As your family completes the exercises in this workbook, a stronger bond will be developed as a direct result of your increasing love for each other. If you think that's impossible ("No one could love his/her family more than I love mine right this moment!"), you may be in for a pleasant surprise. As your intimacy deepens, your knowledge of each other correspondingly deepens. While that may not increase the natural love that God designed parents and children to feel for each other, it gives a new type of love. A new layer. One based not on genetic coding but on learning the depths of each other and forming a bonding friendship.

But no family ever gets to that level of love until they establish firmly the right foundation. And as we've already indicated, that foundation must be a strong and abiding commitment from each family member to the family as a whole and to each person who is a part of that whole.

◆ ◆ ◆

EXERCISE 1:
WHERE IS
YOUR FOCUS?

If your family is headed by two married adults living together in the home, start developing commitment in your family by ensuring commitment to the marriage.[3]

When you married, the person who officiated led you through your vows to each other. The vows may have been the standard ones in the officiant's wedding ceremony, or maybe you wrote them yourself. We know of one couple who literally found theirs on a box of greeting cards! They liked it so much, they cajoled the officiant into incorporating the words into the ceremony.

In this exercise, we'd like for you to write new vows. They will not supersede your earlier vows. You made those before God and man, and they will continue to bind you together, hopefully as long as you both shall live. The vows we ask you to write now will also be binding in a spiritual and emotional sense, if not in a legal sense. Now that you've learned more about each other, know more about what marriage involves, and have a clearer picture of life that isn't always "happily ever after," vows likely will be more practical and more meaningful.

Each of you should write your vows separately from the other. Think of all that you want to promise your spouse, even if you've made the promise a thousand times already. Things like faithfulness, being there for a lifetime, caring, and loving. You may want to include a statement of how you feel about your spouse now and a statement about what you expect to feel for him or her a decade from now. We give you some general guidelines that you may use if you wish.

1. I feel for you:

2. I promise you:

3. I will do for you:

4. Our future will be:

5. What I want most for us is:

6. Our children can count on:

7. I give you:

8. Our spiritual life will be:

9. Our family life will be:

10. I'm committed to:

When you finish jotting ideas for your vows, obtain a nice piece of stationery (a visit to a stationery store may be in order) and write it in your own hand. It makes no difference if your writing style is calligraphy or controlled chaos, writing it instead of typing it makes it more intimate.

If your family chooses the renew your wedding vows activity from the Putting It to Work section, keep your written vows secret from your spouse until the "wedding day." If your family doesn't choose that activity, before this week is over share your vows with each other. Don't exchange them; read them to each other. Or quote them. Together agree to create the right setting and the right time. As the two of you are alone—in a romantic restaurant, on a moonlight cruise, or walking hand in hand on a garden path—open your hearts to each other and renew your vows.

We designed the exercises in this chapter to bring family members closer together. Be aware that as you incorporate younger family members into these exercises, they may react with resentment if the sessions are too long. Therefore, we recommend that you set a maximum time limit (appropriate for your family members' ages and temperaments) for each session. It's better to have two sessions or to slightly speed up a project to finish in a prescribed time limit than to turn these exercises into dreaded drudgery. Have fun! If everyone is enjoying themselves, let a session run longer. Remember, these exercises are made for your family, not your family for these exercises.

◆ ◆ ◆

In your *Fantastic Families* book you read our six characteristics of commitment:

- ◆ Characteristic #1—Commitment to marriage
- ◆ Characteristic #2—Commitment to each individual
- ◆ Characteristic #3—Commitment to putting first things first
- ◆ Characteristic #4—Commitment to honesty
- ◆ Characteristic #5—Commitment to family traditions
- ◆ Characteristic #6—Commitment to the long haul

EXERCISE 2:
THE SIX CHARACTERISTICS OF COMMITMENT

The most difficult commitment for many families is characteristic #3, putting first things first. We have an exercise to help you implement that a little later. But right now, we ask every family member to sign (or make his or her mark if unable to write) The Family Declaration of Commitment, which you'll find on the next page.

We've designed this Declaration so you can make a photocopy of it, frame it, and hang it in a prominent place in your home. However, some families like to create their own documents. You could design the page on a computer, using a fancy font; or if someone in your family has wonderful handwriting or the ablility to do calligraphy, he or she could write the document out by hand—with a Declaration of Independnce look. Either way, you could create the document on premium paper, giving it a distinguished and legal look. If you do create your own document, be sure to leave room at the bottom for every family member to "sign" in his or her fashion.

In a family meeting discuss the implications of the contract and make sure that everyone knows what he or she is committing to. Remind them that the document will be placed where everyone will regularly see it and be reminded of the commitment each family member has to the family and to each member of the family. Ask that no one sign if he or she cannot or will not make this commitment. Everyone needs the assurance that anytime they look at this contract, they will be reminded that the family will be there for each other *no matter what*.

If you wish to alter any of the words of the following contract, please do so without diminishing the commitment.

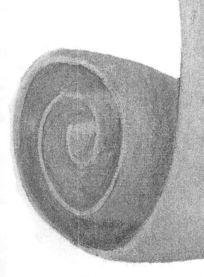

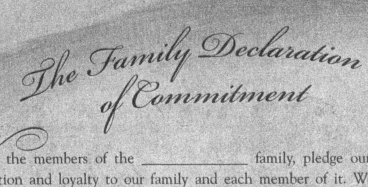

The Family Declaration of Commitment

We, the members of the _____ family, pledge our faithful devotion and loyalty to our family and each member of it. We believe that each family member is precious. We share our lives, our goals, and our values. We commit to complete honesty with each other. We commit to honoring family traditions. We commit to cherishing our family name and keeping it from tarnish. We will be there for each other in good times and bad. We commit to being there for each other when we are needed, both now and forever. We commit to putting family above all those things of life that seem so urgent and demanding but that can never compare to the welfare of our family.

As the children of our family mature and begin families of their own, we commit to support their spouses and children as an extended part of our family. As that progression of life occurs, we pledge that we will encourage each to give primary loyalty to his or her spouse and children. But even as they establish their own families, we will forever hold our dear bond of love and devotion to each other.

We each give our seal below to serve as our word and bond that we will honor all that we have pledged here to each other.

Signed this _____ day of _____
in the year of our Lord _____ .

PUTTING FIRST THINGS FIRST

In a family meeting, the chairperson for that week should appoint a recording secretary. The chairperson instructs the secretary to make clear notes as the family discusses everything that causes any family member to feel that any other family member isn't "putting first things first." The chairperson should open the discussion to the entire group. He or she may say something like, "Okay, our meeting this week is to make sure that we all have our priorities straight. Does anyone feel neglected or lonely because of the schedule or activities of any family member? Or does anyone feel that any of us is spending too much time in some activity that shortchanges the family?"

The chair must ensure the "safety" of every person who speaks. That means that if one family member says something about the too-busy schedule of another family member, that family member can't show any displeasure because of the comment. No negative words, body language, or noises will be allowed. For example, a fourth grader may complain that Dad travels too much and that she misses him terribly. Dad cannot in any way make her feel bad that she has expressed her feelings on the matter. Neither is he to defend himself. At this time the family is only trying to get everything on the floor; discussion will come later.

When everyone has shared his or her thoughts on this matter, the secretary should categorize and read the matters to be discussed. If more than one family member is unhappy with Dad's travel, the secretary compiles all those into one statement. As the secretary reads each statement, the chair asks how many family members feel this way. The secretary tallies the votes. (This should give all the family a clearer picture as to whether this feeling is isolated to one family member or common to many members.)

After the vote on each issue, the family together discusses the problem and brainstorms solutions to the problem. The group doesn't have to resolve the issue in this meeting; some things take time to reorder. The goal is to understand the problem, understand the reasons the problem exists, understand the consequences to the individual whose priorities are questioned if he or she were to reorder them, understand the impact that reordering will have on the family as a whole, and to give brainstorming suggestions as to how to resolve the issue.

We outline the entire process for you below:

1. Elect a chairperson (if this job isn't already assigned by regular rotation) who then appoints the recording secretary.

2. The chair opens the meeting to comments from any family member who feels that another is neglecting the family because of misplaced priorities.

3. The chair ensures the safety of all who speak and makes it clear that there are to be no negative responses or personal defenses.

4. The secretary categorizes all the statements and reads each category aloud.

5. After each category is read, the family votes to show how many members believe this really is a misplaced priority that should be corrected.

6. The chair leads a discussion for the resolution of that specific problem.

   ◆ Understand the problem.

   ◆ Understand the reasons the problem exists.

   ◆ Understand the consequences to the individual whose priorities are questioned, if he or she were to reorder this priority.

   ◆ Understand the impact that reordering will have on the family as a whole.

   ◆ Brainstorm suggestions as to how to resolve the issue.

Remember that it may take a few family meetings to resolve all the issues.

Putting It to Work—Six Ideas for Your Family

In the *Fantastic Families* book, we end chapter 1 by giving six ideas that your family can use to foster commitment to each other.

1. Have periodic family councils.
2. Renew your wedding vows.
3. Rearrange your schedules.
4. Examine your marriage relationship for danger signs.
5. Read good books as a family.
6. Rent movies that deal with commitment.

In this chapter and each to follow, we ask you to choose one of the "Putting It to Work" activities that involves the entire family. Then you must commit to beginning that activity during this calendar week!

For the best results, have the entire family vote on the activity to do. Allow plenty of discussion and campaigning. That will be fun. Do *not* allow any cajoling, crying, or pouting. That will surely create *less* family harmony, not more. If anyone acts in that fashion, he or she will lose voting rights for this week. Tell the entire family this when the meeting starts, and you're likely to have a much better meeting!

1. HAVE PERIODIC FAMILY COUNCILS

If you choose having periodic family councils as your activity, those councils should be more comprehensive than the family meetings you are having to do these exercises. Run more like the "town meetings" of New England, a family council gives each family member a say in the "governing" of the family. (Of course, there should be certain unalterable rules that cannot be transcended by family council. For example, the kids cannot depose mother and father and adopt new parents!) If your family votes to begin regular family councils, the parent(s) should establish guidelines for those meetings, considering these questions:

- How often will we have the meetings?
- What type issues may be voted on and what type issues are solely in parental domain?
- How will each family member have a fair say and an equal vote?
- What veto or overriding power will the parent(s) have, and how do we make that very clear before the first family council?
- How much are we *really* willing to allow our children to have a say in what our family does?
- What infractions, if any, preclude a family member from voting, and when would he or she have the right to vote again?

2. Renew Your Wedding Vows

If the family chooses this activity, allow everyone in on the planning. (The planning has to start this week, but the renewing of vows can be done whenever the family decides.) Decide how formal or informal, who to invite, when to have it, where to have it, who will officiate (the person doesn't have to be licensed for this), what kind of party or reception should follow. If the group decides on a simple route, make all decisions together. If it winds up being quite an affair, delegate specific family members for specific tasks. (One word of caution: Make budgets and spending limits *very* clear at the outset, or enthusiastic family members may create havoc.)

3. Rearrange Your Schedules

If your family chooses this activity, we recommend that you approach it as described in exercise 2.

4. Examine Your Marriage Relationship for Danger Signs

We suggest that you avoid this as a family project unless you have only teens and they are very mature. In that case, they may actually give you profound insight into your marital relationship and how you can make it better. But if you can't cope with marriage advice from your children, or if the process of having them think about it will cause stress or anxiety, work on this one without the kids.

5. Read Good Books as a Family

Your family may choose to make one evening each week the book evening. No television, phone off the hook, sign on the door telling folks to quietly tiptoe away. Assign different family members to read different books aloud to the family. Your six year old may get through two books in a one-hour session. Your senior in high school may take six weeks to guide you through *The Adventures of Tom Sawyer*. We suggest you reserve the last half-hour of your session to discuss what has been read. (A word of advice: Make sure you know the content of each book and think through how its content will affect *each* family member.)

6. RENT MOVIES THAT DEAL WITH COMMITMENT

Movie night obviously takes more time than book night. An hour of reading aloud taxes most voices. Many movies are at least one and a half hours long—some longer. Some simply entertain. Some require serious family discussions at the end as you explore meanings, lessons to be learned, and make real life applications. If you choose this activity, allow plenty of time for it. Also make it fun. Rather than starting with the movie, you may want to begin with community popcorn popping or grilling burgers in the backyard. (Think through the effect of the movie on each family member *before* watching the movie together.)

DECIDING WHICH ACTIVITY THE FAMILY WILL PURSUE

In either a formal family meeting or an informal meeting (everyone around the dinner table as a meal ends), that week's chairperson should announce the six activities and call for a discussion.

Each person may address which activity he or she wants the family to do and give reasons why. After each has spoken, the family votes on any of the six that have been spoken about. (If no one wanted to do an activity, you naturally exclude it from the voting.)

When the activity has been chosen, decide when the family will begin. If the activity is the renewing of the wedding vows, set a time to have the first organizational meeting. Tell people to come up with ideas before the meeting. If it is a book or movie night, assign the person who will choose and read the first book or choose the first movie. Explain that parents must approve all choices before they're actually brought to the group for presentation.

HELPING OTHERS

The following chart gives general age-level characteristics from the Family/School/Community Partnership, A Model for Strengthening Families, Executive Summary.[4] They used this chart for parents and teachers to have a guideline for goals and exercises for each age group they worked with. You may use it in the same way. After reading it, you likely will have more specific ideas for what you should expect from each child and what you would like to accomplish with each child. Following the chart you'll find a few suggestions for using this chart with members of your family.

Commitment

- ◆ Sharing roles and responsibilities
- ◆ Establishing and maintaining priorities
- ◆ Establishing traditions and rituals
- ◆ Maintaining relationships
- ◆ Finding mutual support

Prenatal/Birth	Infancy
Marriage	Trusting Environment
Prenatal Care	Consistent care
	Making family life important

Preschool–Kindergarten	Kindergarten–Grade 3
Enriching environment	Print-rich environment (books, magazines, etc.)
Learning gender identity	Socializing for individual/family roles
Sharing time, friends, possessions	Helping with family celebrations
Celebrating family traditions	Relating emotionally to nonfamily adults
Relating emotionally to parents/grandparents	

Grades 4–5	Grades 6–8
Supportive environment	Positive learning environment
Sharing home responsibilities	Identifying family roles and responsibilities
Recognizing cultural traditions	Challenges of the dual career family
Relating emotionally to peers	Becoming industrious
Developing initiative	Demonstrating care of others
Wholesome after-school activities	Accepting cultural differences
	Mutual respect and appreciation

Grades 9–12	Early Adult
Stable environment	Making career decisions
Managing home responsibilities	Seeking and verifying one's mate and friends; marriage
Interfacing rights/ responsibilities	Bonding with lifetime friends
Accepting social responsibility	Clarifying roles and values
Establishing personal identity	Accepting responsibility
Sharing intimacy/feelings	Sharing family caring
Committing to life goals	

Middle Adult	Later Adult
Changing family functions regarding negotiating and changing rules	Parenting grandchildren
Redefining values	Investing for grandchildren
Advocating for self, family, and communities	Supporting changes of job, retirement, health, location
Empowering self to make better families	Commitment to keep growing and learning
Accepting responsibility	Positive role modeling
Recognizing the interrelatedness of family and society	Commitment to passing on skills and values
	Commitment to share family customs and continuity
	Commitment to future generations

WAYS TO INVOLVE EVERYONE

We believe that with a little creativity, you can find ways to involve every person in your household in the exercises in this chapter and following chapters. The previous ideas should stimulate ideas in your own mind as to how.

For example, they suggest you can help children kindergarten–grade 3 by giving them a print-rich environment. If your family chose to have book nights in "Putting It to Work," make sure each time that you include a ten- to fifteen-minute section where you read a book to your children in that age group. Have younger children hold the book, tell you what the pictures are about, etc. Have children who can read share a book from their level. Make sure that all family members pay close attention, no matter what the age of the children, and reward them with words, applause, and hugs, so that they feel a sense of belonging and accomplishment.

Let's look at another example, such as the renewing wedding vows activity. The chart suggests that children in grades 4–5 can learn more commitment by recognizing cultural traditions. What better way to involve a child in that age group than by giving all the details of your original wedding? If it was in a church, explain why. If the bride wore white, explain that tradition. If there was a special aspect to your ceremony based on your religious beliefs, explain that too.

One of the suggestions for preschool–kindergartners is sharing time, friends, and possessions. Involving a child of that age in family meetings, teaching him or her to wait, to listen, and to speak only during his or her turn would accomplish that quite well.

Of course, there are ways to involve every child from every age group in any exercise in this chapter. We only illustrate one or two to get your creativity cranked.

We know that you will have a great time working through these exercises. We also know that as you do, your family will grow in many wonderful ways—becoming a stronger unit, learning each other's feelings, and inviting each person's valuable contributions.

In the next chapter, it gets even better.

STEP TWO
EXPRESS APPRECIATION
AND AFFECTION

Maybe we notice it more when it doesn't happen than when it does. When we hear "thank you" we may respond with a humble "no problem," the American version of the Spanish response *de nada*, "it's nothing." But it *is* something when an expected expression of gratitude goes unshared.

"He didn't even have the courtesy to thank me for picking up the tab at lunch."

"Nobody around here seems to appreciate what I do. It's like I'm a slave who's expected to serve *them* hand and foot."

"Well, that's the last time I do a favor for her. Why should I do something nice for her when she apparently takes it for granted?"

People who feel that way aren't petty. They're normal. Even God wants to be thanked for what he does for us. Jesus once healed ten lepers, and only one returned to thank him. Did he notice the slight?

> Jesus asked, "Were not all ten cleansed? Where are the other nine? Was no one found to return and give praise to God except this foreigner?" Then he said to him, "Rise and go; your faith has made you well."[1]

We can imagine a mom empathizing with Jesus after washing and drying four loads of laundry, cooking, cleaning the kitchen, and finally dropping exhausted onto the sofa next to her teenaged daughter who mumbles, "Mom, bring me some popcorn and a Coke." Mom might react by thinking, "Have you not noticed all I've done for you? And here you are, not offering to bring me anything, demanding that I serve you some more? What thanks do I get for all I do for you?" If she were to phrase her thoughts in words similar to Jesus, she would say, "Is no one found to return and give praise?"

Breadwinners feel unappreciated when other family members take his or her contribution to family welfare for granted. Kids feel it when they work hard for a good grade and get only a distracted "that's nice" from a disinterested parent. Homemakers feel it when offers of help come few and far between and pleas for assistance fall defeated under a barrage of "I can't help you right now because I have to..."

Strong families understand the tremendous desire every human carries for appreciation. They also know that the most effective appreciation always dresses itself in layers of affection. A perfunctory thank you covers the basics of nicety. A thank you wrapped in a hug and a squeeze makes a delightful gift to be relished.

When a family constantly incorporates appreciation and affection into their daily interactions, they affect the entire atmosphere of the home. The warmth and gentleness created make a powerful barrier against tension, anger, and self-ishness. Everything becomes more pleasant because everyone feels not only accepted but treasured. Every relationship benefits.

◆ ◆ ◆

EXERCISE 1:
LEARNING HOW TO SHOW APPRECIATION AND AFFECTION

As in other chapters, we designed this first exercise for adults. You may involve mature children if you wish. We believe that if you master the ability to freely express appreciation and to freely give affection, younger children in your home will learn that skill from you.

If you already do these two things well, wonderful! But believing that you do it well doesn't necessarily mean that you do. Forgive us if we seem cynical, but we've noticed that many people who think they are quite good at something make that assessment subjectively when there is usually a way to make it more objectively.

For example, in Family Dynamics's *His Needs, Her Needs* eight-week interactive course, we ask couples to rate each other on several important matters. When Joe and Alice Beam took the course several years ago, they completed the evaluation for affection just like every other couple in the class, even though Joe had written the course. When they shared their scores, Joe saw with utter disbelief that Alice had given him a –2 on affection! When he shares that story with audiences today, he says, "I immediately explained to her that she must have misunderstood the questions!"

He then continues, "What I thought were clear expressions of affection weren't communicating affection at all as far as Alice was concerned. I finally had to ask, 'What do *you* want me to do to demonstrate my affection for you?' As I listened, I learned that truly expressing affection isn't accomplished by having the right *intention*, it's by doing the right *action*. You *must* show it in a way that the other person interprets as affection."

The first step of this exercise is to start by rating each other. (We won't use the scale with negative numbers, so you won't suffer the same shock that Joe did.) Begin with husband and wife. Then do the same exercise with children mature enough to answer the questions honestly. *If a child lacks self-confidence or could in any way be hurt by being rated, don't rate him or her at this time.* You may, however, allow all children who are mature enough to understand the questions rate every adult in the family.

Follow these three rules for this exercise:

1. Give each person rating you permission to tell you the absolute truth without fear of any kind of negative reaction (no anger, arguing, cajoling, pouting, withdrawing, withholding, etc.).

2. Children who are mature enough to understand the statements may participate in rating the parent(s).

3. Only children designated by the parent(s) may be rated by anyone— parent or child. *The parent(s) should designate* only *those children who are mature enough to react positively to being rated!*

To ensure that you can explain the ratings you give below, please write your own definitions or descriptions of appreciation and affection. When you discuss your ratings with your spouse, child, or parent, start by giving your definitions of appreciation and affection.

Maybe Webster's definition will help you more clearly state yours:

Appreciation: gratitude; thankful recognition...the act of estimating the qualities of things and giving them their proper value...clear perception or recognition.[2]

Affection: fond attachment, devotion, or love...emotion; feeling; sentiment...the emotional realm of love.[3]

Dr. Willard Harley further describes affection in *Five Steps to Romantic Love* as:

Showing love through words, cards, gifts, hugs, kisses, and courtesies; creating an environment that clearly and repeatedly expresses love.[4]

1. Write here your ideas about what *appreciation* is and how it should be shown:

2. Now write your ideas about what *affection* is and how it should be shown:

Now it's time for you to give ratings to others in your family.

RATING APPRECIATION AND AFFECTION FROM MY SPOUSE

Use this seven-point scale to rate the following statements.

1—extremely dissatisfied
2—very dissatisfied
3—somewhat dissatisfied
4—mixed
5—somewhat satisfied
6—very satisfied
7—extremely satisfied

1. I am satisfied with the quantity of appreciation I receive from my spouse.

_____

If you give a score of 5 or less, please explain why you feel the way you do about not getting enough appreciation.

2. I am satisfied with the way(s) my spouse shows me appreciation. _____

If you give a score of 5 or less, please write here the ways you want your spouse to show you appreciation.

3. I am satisfied with the quantity of affection I receive from my spouse.

_____

If you give a score of 5 or less, please explain why you feel the way you do about not getting enough affection.

4. I am satisfied with the way(s) my spouse shows me affection. _____

If you give a score of 5 or less, please write here the ways you want your spouse to show you affection.

When each spouse has finished this exercise, share your definitions and scores with each other. Be more interested in listening than defending, in learning than explaining. If you open yourself to being taught by your spouse, you may just open a new world of intimacy with each other.

RATING APPRECIATION AND AFFECTION FROM MY FATHER

Use this seven-point scale to rate the following statements.

1—extremely dissatisfied
2—very dissatisfied
3—somewhat dissatisfied
4—mixed
5—somewhat satisfied
6—very satisfied
7—extremely satisfied

1. I am satisfied with the quantity of appreciation I receive from my father.

_____

If you give a score of 5 or less, please explain why you feel the way you do about not getting enough appreciation.

2. I am satisfied with the way(s) my father shows me appreciation. _____

If you give a score of 5 or less, please write here the ways you want your father to show you appreciation.

3. I am satisfied with the quantity of affection I receive from my father.

_____

If you give a score of 5 or less, please explain why you feel the way you do about not getting enough affection.

4. I am satisfied with the way(s) my father shows me affection. _____

If you give a score of 5 or less, please write here the ways you want your father to show you affection.

When finished, share your definitions and scores with your father.

RATING APPRECIATION AND AFFECTION FROM MY MOTHER

Use this seven-point scale to rate the following statements.
1—extremely dissatisfied
2—very dissatisfied
3—somewhat dissatisfied
4—mixed
5—somewhat satisfied
6—very satisfied
7—extremely satisfied

1. I am satisfied with the quantity of appreciation I receive from my mother.

_____

If you give a score of 5 or less, please explain why you feel the way you do about not getting enough appreciation.

2. I am satisfied with the way(s) my mother shows me appreciation.

_____

If you give a score of 5 or less, please write here the ways you want your mother to show you appreciation.

3. I am satisfied with the quantity of affection I receive from my mother.
_____

If you give a score of 5 or less, please explain why you feel the way you do about not getting enough affection.

4. I am satisfied with the way(s) my mother shows me affection. _____

If you give a score of 5 or less, please write here the ways you want your mother to show you affection.

When finished, share your definitions and scores with your mother.

Now, parent(s), we give you forms to rate two children. Don't use them if you have no children who meet the criteria given at the beginning of this exercise. If you have more than two children who meet the criteria, use extra paper.

RATING APPRECIATION AND AFFECTION FROM MY CHILD

Use this seven-point scale to rate the following statements.

1—extremely dissatisfied
2—very dissatisfied
3—somewhat dissatisfied
4—mixed
5—somewhat satisfied
6—very satisfied
7—extremely satisfied

1. I am satisfied with the quantity of appreciation I receive from
_____. _____

If you give a score of 5 or less, please explain why you feel the way you do about not getting enough appreciation.

2. I am satisfied with the way(s) _____ shows me appreciation. _____

If you give a score of 5 or less, please write here the ways you want _____ to show you appreciation.

3. I am satisfied with the quantity of affection I receive from
_____. _____

If you give a score of 5 or less, please explain why you feel the way you do about not getting enough affection.

4. I am satisfied with the way(s) _____ shows me affection.
_____

If you give a score of 5 or less, please write here the ways you want _____ to show you affection.

When finished, share your definitions and scores with this child:_____.

RATING APPRECIATION AND AFFECTION FROM MY CHILD

Use this seven-point scale to rate the following statements.

1—extremely dissatisfied
2—very dissatisfied
3—somewhat dissatisfied
4—mixed
5—somewhat satisfied
6—very satisfied
7—extremely satisfied

1. I am satisfied with the quantity of appreciation I receive from
_____. _____

If you give a score of 5 or less, please explain why you feel the way you do about not getting enough appreciation.

2. I am satisfied with the way(s) _____ shows me appreciation. _____

If you give a score of 5 or less, please write here the ways you want _____ to show you appreciation.

3. I am satisfied with the quantity of affection I receive from
_____. _____

If you give a score of 5 or less, please explain why you feel the way you do about not getting enough affection.

4. I am satisfied with the way(s) _____ shows me affection.
_____

If you give a score of 5 or less, please write here the ways you want
_____ to show you affection.

When finished, share your definitions and scores with this child:_____.

MAKING CHANGES

As we wrote in *Fantastic Families*, there may be many reasons that a person
has difficulty in showing appreciation and affection. If you were rated a five or
lower on any of the evaluations given to you by spouse or children, you may need
to do some introspection to figure out why. If you find it impossible to give the
appreciation or affection your family needs, consider therapy with a professional
who can help you find the root and the cure for your inability.

Most who score low won't need therapy, just a plan. Like Joe Beam discov-
ered several years ago in the *His Needs, Her Needs* course, sometimes the solution
is as simple as learning to communicate in words and actions meaningful to the
other person. That's why it is so important to know how each person defines
appreciation and affection—what they expect, need, or desire from you. If you
each operate with a different understanding of what appreciation or affection is,
you won't understand each other's actions.

Listen carefully when a spouse, child, or parent explains why he or she scored
you low, and hear very clearly what they want from you. When you know what
that is, do it. Yes, that's right. Just do it! It doesn't matter if you feel awkward at
the outset. What matters is that you genuinely want to fulfill the needs of your
family. It's not hypocritical to do something other than what you feel; it's only
hypocritical if you don't care what they feel.

Write a plan here that you will pledge to yourself and God that you will fulfill by giving appreciation and affection to each member of your family.

For _____ I will:

For _____ I will:

For _____ I will:

For _____ I will:

> **W**e designed the exercises in this chapter to bring family members closer together. Be aware that as you incorporate younger family members into these exercises, they may react with resentment if the sessions are too long. Therefore, we recommend that you set a maximum time limit (appropriate for your family members' ages and temperaments) for each session. It's better to have two sessions or to slightly speed up a project to finish in a prescribed time limit than to turn these exercises into dreaded drudgery. Have fun! If everyone is enjoying themselves, let a session run longer. Remember, these exercises are made for your family, not your family for these exercises.

In the *Fantastic Families* book we discuss six secrets to cultivating appreciation and affection in your home.

EXERCISE 2: USING THE SIX SECRETS FOR CULTIVATING APPRECIATION AND AFFECTION IN YOUR HOME

Secret #1—Dig for diamonds. (Look for the good in each person.)

Secret #2—Affirm your children verbally. (Say it!)

Secret #3—Expect children to be affectionate and appreciative.
(People tend to do what is expected of them.)

Secret #4—Share humor and playfulness.
(A fun atmosphere promotes good feelings.)

Secret #5—Purposely encourage affection and appreciation.
(Point out to others when someone should be affirmed.)

Secret #6—Accept expressions of appreciation gracefully.
(Make people feel good that they gave you a compliment.)

THE APPRECIATION GAME

This game incorporates all of the six secrets just listed . It's a fun game to play anytime the family is together in a casual setting. The Beam family enjoys playing it in the car as they travel. Playing it over dinner or while lounging around the patio in the backyard would work just as well. All that you need is the proximity where everyone can hear and the patience to let the game proceed at a natural, unforced pace. You can even center your family meeting this week around this game.

1. The gamemaster (selected by the parent[s]) chooses one family member as the first recipient.

2. Everyone takes turns completing this one statement about the recipient: "One thing I like about you is…"

3. The recipient must reply with thankful or appreciative words only. He or she may not elaborate, disagree, question, or anything else. The best reply is "thank you very much."

4. When everyone finishes completing the statement about recipient one, the gamemaster moves to recipient two—a family member of his or her choosing.

5. Every family member takes turns as the recipient until all family members have been included. The last recipient is the gamemaster.

6. When the first round is completed, other rounds follow as time allows. Choose from these statements:

   ◆ One good thing about you I've never told you is…

   ◆ Something I really appreciate about you is…

   ◆ A nice thing I've heard someone say about you is…

   ◆ One way that I wish I were more like you is…

   ◆ I find you loveable because…

   ◆ I like the way you show affection by…

   ◆ I'm glad you're my (spouse, parent, child, brother, sister, aunt, uncle) because…

   ◆ I will show you more affection by…

   ◆ If I could have one wish come true for you, it would be…

To complete this exercise for this chapter, you must do it at least once this week. If you want to create and nourish an atmosphere of appreciation and affection, make it a ritual that occurs every time you do a particular thing. For example, it could become the routine on the way to church on Sunday mornings. It could be the game you play every time you travel. You could even make a short version of it as the routine way you say goodnight to each other every night.

Try it; you'll like it.

Putting It to Work—Six Ideas for Your Family

The *Fantastic Families* book lists six ideas at the end of chapter 2 that your family can use.

1. Write down ten things you like about your spouse.
2. Create a positive, pleasant environment in your home.
3. Try reframing the situation.
4. Encourage appreciation by receiving it gracefully.
5. Give one compliment per day to your spouse and kids.
6. Write birthday letters expressing your love.

Each of these is explained or described briefly in the text of the book. Before this week is over, we strongly urge your family to take a vote on which of the six should become a priority this week. Whatever idea you choose, you must begin it this week!

If any of these six will help your family achieve the goal set in the introduction session, choose that activity. The above six activities are further explained below.

1. WRITE DOWN TEN THINGS YOU LIKE ABOUT YOUR SPOUSE/ WRITE BIRTHDAY LETTERS EXPRESSING YOUR LOVE

Odds are against you that each person in your family celebrates a birthday this week. If you are, happy birthday! If you're not, why not combine these two suggested activities into one.

Ask family members to write a letter to every other member of the family expressing love to or an admirable quality in that person. (Older kids can help younger kids—even to the point of asking them questions and writing their answers for them.) To make it more fun, go by a stationery store if you can and buy a box of blank cards and envelopes. Distribute them so that every person has a card and envelope for every other person. Decide which day all letters must be turned in to the postmaster (the chairperson for this week). When the family meeting takes place, the chair shuffles the envelopes and distributes them to all family members who can read. One at a time each card is opened, read so that the entire group can hear, and then given to the author so that he or she may hand deliver the card to the person to whom they wrote it.

As the session ends, the group agrees that on each person's birthday, they will all read similar cards they will have written to the birthday person. One person should be elected to remind everyone within two weeks of each birthday to write the card that is due.

2. CREATE A POSITIVE, PLEASANT ENVIRONMENT IN YOUR HOME

This describes a result more than it does an activity. If your family chooses this option, we recommend that you have a group discussion about what a positive, pleasant environment would be like. Describe specific things that would happen or exist. Describe specific things that would NOT happen and how they could be avoided. Keep talking until you all have a measurable way of knowing when you would have reached this objective. When you agree, write it down and keep it in an obvious place. (Perhaps laminate it and keep it on the coffee table or on the refrigerator so that anyone can read it at any time.) When family members do things to help create this environment, show appreciation to each other both verbally and physically (hugs, kisses, high-fives).

3. TRY REFRAMING THE SITUATION

Reframing is a slightly different version of the game we encouraged in exercise 2. In reframing, one doesn't look for the positive qualities in a person, but those that appear to be not so positive. The object isn't to reinforce negative or antisocial behavior. Instead, it's to help each person see the good that can be found in his or her weaker or less attractive traits. If a person—adult or child—can see the positive in him- or herself, often the behaviors can be gradually modified to be more helpful than harmful.

If your family chooses this option, approach it carefully. A mature, caring adult may be able to see that a domineering and bossy child could be reframed so that he or she is viewed as one who is learning leadership skills. Other kids in the house may think you're crazy if you say that! "Leadership? Ego is what it is!" Even worse, they may think you're allowing that child to get away with things that you would never let them do. No one wants a bossy child, and if your reframing helps him or her overcome the bossiness and learn true leadership, you'll do well. But if you inadvertently encourage the bossiness, everyone in the family will suffer until you get the message straightened out!

Reframing is a great way to help others see the positive in a negative situation. Just make sure that both parents and children have a good grasp on the purpose and methodology before trying it on any kind of regular basis.

4. GIVE ONE COMPLIMENT A DAY/ ENCOURAGE APPRECIATION BY RECEIVING IT GRACEFULLY

These two activities blend nicely into one. If your family chooses it, we recommend that you don't set a specific time to give and receive compliments like you would in the Appreciation Game in exercise 2. Instead, let each person give his or her compliment to other family members when he or she sees the opportunity. This will encourage everyone to be especially watchful to catch other family members doing something nice. At the end of each day, you may want to get a recap in a brief, informal way: "Sally, what were you complimented on today?"

To model this correctly, the parent(s) *must* find some compliment to give to every person in the family on every single day. And to teach your children how to accept compliments, pay close attention to your responses when a child compliments you. Don't ignore it or mumble a distracted thank you. Look the child in the eye and make him or her feel good that they complimented you. Thank him or her for the compliment and then tell how receiving the compliment made you feel. "Why, thank you, Sally. I was hoping someone would notice my new tie. That makes me feel good."

Keep this up for a while, and your entire household will become a happier home.

HELPING OTHERS

As in other chapters, we end this one with a chart that may help you get ideas as to how to incorporate every person in your family in this week's topic.

As you read through the chart, you'll see that the exercises we give in this chapter can be adapted to every age group. For example, the Appreciation Game in exercise 2 will help preschool–kindergarten children learn social cognition skills, just as it will help those in grades 4–5 learn to recognize others for doing a good job.

Instead of giving specific ways to apply this chart as we did in the previous chapter, we leave the application to you. The chart can help prevent you from expecting too much, or too little, from your children. We include it as a guide to help you find the general approach for each child so that you can be both challenging and encouraging. Nothing is more discouraging—even to very young children—than to have demands placed on us that we cannot meet. And nothing insults us more than to be given tasks beneath our abilities.

We're sure you'll know just what to do for every person in your family.

By the way, don't forget to read what is written on the chart for adults. They, too, need self-esteem (note Middle Adult) and can benefit from playing the Appreciation Game (with Later Adults sharing thoughts and feelings in intergenerational settings).

The next chapter will get into more detail about how family members can communicate with each other.

Appreciation and Affection

- ◆ Caring for self and others
- ◆ Respecting privacy
- ◆ Maintaining positive attitudes, compliments, and rewards
- ◆ Enjoying the environment

Prenatal/Birth	Infancy
Respect/affection	Accepting individual uniqueness/needs
Extending family support	Loving, caring adults

Preschool–Kindergarten	Kindergarten–Grade 3
Caring for belongings	Self-help skills
Social cognition skills	Respecting self and others
Setting limits	Respecting ownership of possessions
Positive self-image	Positive attitudes toward learning
Family outings	Learning about the environment
Environmental awareness	Saving resources
	Field trips

Grades 4–5	Grades 6–8
Respecting individual differences	Accepting self, grooming
Sex equity	Respecting civil rights of others
Respecting space needs of each family member	Respecting property
Recognizing others for doing a good job	Demonstrating qualities that are appreciated by others
Learning about community helpers	Community service projects
	Protecting natural environment

Grades 9–12	Early Adult
Allocating family resources	Establishing philosophical basis for ethical, political, and moral decisions
Volunteering	Accepting self-imposed limits
Responsible citizenship	Establishing healthy lifestyle
Accepting limits	Initiating citizen involvement
Showing appreciation	Accepting appreciation
Environmental issues	Fostering self-determination
	Enjoying environment

Middle Adult	Later Adult
Independence vs. dependence	Sharing thoughts and feelings in intergenerational settings
Gaining or regaining self-esteem	Accepting differences between the generations
Continuing self-care	Tolerating and coping with different values
Understanding adult stages of life	Awareness of others' needs
Accepting psychological changes	Appreciation and acceptance of the limitations of others
Recognizing individual differences	Appreciation for producers
Participating in community improvement	
Protecting the environment	

STEP THREE
SHARE POSITIVE COMMUNICATION

It's usually the first answer we hear fervently emphasized in any Family Dynamics's marriage seminar. As quickly as we ask, "What do you hope to gain from this seminar?" the answer echoes instantly, "Communication. Teach us how to communicate."

We don't just hear it from husbands or wives; we hear it from parents too. "Something's wrong. I speak; my kids look at the floor. I ask; they mumble if they make any reply at all. If I try to make a joke to relieve tension; they roll their eyes. Is there any such thing as communicating with your kids when they've crossed into the twilight zone?"

Interestingly, the complaint doesn't reside in the realm of adults only. We hear it from kids as well. "Can you do something to my mom and dad so that they, like, know that I have feelings and ideas and stuff too? They want to do all the talking and none of the listening. When I try to tell them something, they're on my back before I get halfway through what I'm trying to say. It's like they have all the answers, you know, without even knowing what the real question is."

If you spent much time listening to people like we do in our seminars, you likely would conclude that the average family does much more talking (talking may be too nice a word for it) than genuinely communicating. Communication means more than whispering, saying, or bellowing one's thoughts, feelings, or wishes for the world to hear and heed. According to Webster's unabridged dictionary:

> **Communicate:** to impart knowledge of; make known...to share in or partake of...to give or interchange thoughts, feelings, information, or the like by writing, speaking, etc.... to express thoughts, feelings, or information easily or effectively.[1]

> **Communication:** the imparting or interchange of thoughts, opinions, or information by speech, writing, or signs.[2]

Did you notice the key word in the two definitions from Webster's? No, not the word *impart*. That aspect *is* important without doubt, but imparting information may or may not fulfill the goal of communication. For example, Joe Beam once sat in a college group's devotional in Bangkok and listened for an hour as a Thai preacher taught in his native tongue from the Bible. A lot of imparting took place—plenty of words, gestures, inflection, and so on—but no communication occurred between the preacher and Joe. (Joe claims he had a similar experience in a statistics class in graduate school in Indiana.)

To our way of thinking, the most important word in the definitions above is *interchange*. True communication occurs only when the person receiving the message understands clearly the thought that the sender meant to give. When that happens, the communicator does what Webster's says: He "makes known" his thoughts, and the person being communicated to can "share in" or "partake of" those thoughts.

Let's consider a couple of examples. A wife may explain for years how important it is that her husband treats her with respect and affection. But if he is unaware of *her* understandings about respect or affection, she will not receive from him what she longs for. On the other hand, he may tell her for years how he needs more admiration. If she perceives admiration differently than he does, her best efforts toward fulfilling him will fail miserably. Both will be frustrated.

That's why in the previous chapter we had you write your own definitions of appreciation and affection and then share those definitions with each other. You can't get from the other person what you desire if you cannot communicate to him or her a clear understanding of what that desire is. As the old saying goes, "You can talk till you're blue in the face, and it won't get you anywhere."

So how do people communicate clearly? Is it as simple as defining everything and then explaining the definitions? And if it is, do we really have to go around defining everything for the rest of our lives?

No. And yes.

No one wants to have to explain every thought or feeling as if talking with a three year old. But everyone wants to be understood. We believe we have a happy balance in our model of communication. It doesn't operate on the level of a three-year-old child, but it does call for a straightforward method of understanding.

THE SIX-STEP COMMUNICATION MODEL

Allow us to introduce a model for communication developed by Joe Beam.[3] (We ask in advance that communications experts forgive any oversimplification.) We present the following six-step model to help us more effectively communicate about communication.

The Communication Model

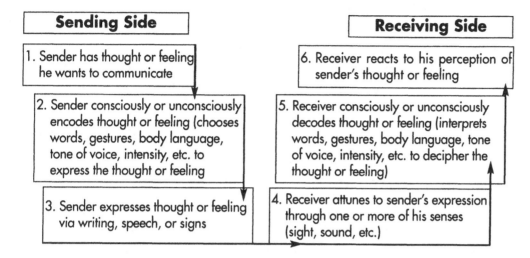

Within the above model, there are only six points in the communication process where communication can fail.

"Only six!" you may note. "There are just six steps in the model!"

We're glad you're paying attention.

Miscommunication can occur during *any* of the above steps. Even worse, any step done poorly usually causes succeeding steps to be ineffective as well.

FAILURE DURING STEP ONE

Think for a moment how communication could fail at the very first step. Suppose a wife becomes distraught during a day in which nothing worked as she expected. No one item in particular distressed her; she just reaches the end of her day feeling overwhelmed and anxious. If the wife wants to communicate to her husband that she's upset, but she herself isn't yet clear about why she is upset or exactly what it is that she feels, the first step of the process fails. Her trying to communicate by following steps 2–6 probably won't lead to a clear interchange of information with her husband. Why? Because if she isn't sure of what she feels, how can she "encode" those confused feelings into words, body language, and the like that will clearly express her feelings to him? Her attempt to express her confused feelings to her husband will likely be garbled on her side—the sending side—of the model. If that happens, it's a good chance the message will continue to be garbled on his side—the receiving side—of the communication model. As he receives her message and tries to interpret it, he may correctly conclude that she is distraught, but the message about *why* she is feeling that way won't be clear to him at all. As he tries to interpret, he may decide she's angry with him and become defensive. Or he could conclude that she's overreacting to some minor situation and ignore her distress. He may even write her communication off as "some woman thing beyond my comprehension" and become distressed himself. If he misinterprets her expressions, his reaction will clearly demonstrate that he *doesn't* understand, making her feel even more distraught. That may well escalate the conversation into new and unexpected negative territory.

Does that mean that one person in a family shouldn't talk to another unless he or she has clearly deciphered personal thoughts or feelings? No. Sometimes the most effective communication between people in a family occurs when one actually clarifies his or her thinking while conversing with another family member. We'll later show you how to do that—how step 1 can be modified to create good communication. For now, we continue explaining how a poorly done step causes other steps to be poorly done.

FAILURE DURING STEP TWO

Even when the thoughts or feelings in step 1 are clear, choosing the wrong encoding in step 2 will corrupt the communication process anyway. Suppose, for example, that a child attempts to communicate to his mother what to him is a clear thought, but his limited vocabulary causes him to choose the wrong words to encode that thought. (What parent hasn't had this experience?) The child expresses the thought in what he believes to be a clear manner, but the mother interprets the child's words incorrectly because of the different meaning they carry for her. Can you imagine a young child exclaiming, "Look at the fire in the backyard!" and his mother flying to the window in panic only to discover the backyard full of fireflies dotting the evening sky? One word, *fire*, carrying two meanings. The young child somehow forgetting the *fly* part in the name of that neat little bug; the mother fearing her favorite tree is flaming to the heavens. Two very different concepts based on the differing understanding of one little word.

Even when the right words are chosen, the nonverbals—body language, tone of voice, etc.—can alter the interpretation made by the other words. A husband aggravated with a malfunctioning television remote control comes to bed and responds to his wife's cooed, "I love you," with those same words from himself in a tone of voice that says something quite different. He does love her; it's the remote control he doesn't like. There likely would be several minutes of frosty conversation before he convinced her of that.

Dressing the right words with the wrong accessories is like walking into a formal banquet wearing a bikini. Everyone takes note, but no one knows the appropriate response.

Some professional speakers used to claim that 7 percent of communication takes place in the words that we choose, 38 percent in the tone of voice with which we present those words, and 55 percent in the nonverbals, such as body language, that accompany the words. Whether the percentages are accurate or not, the principle certainly appears to be true. The person we communicate to is interpreting much more than just the words that we say.

FAILURE DURING STEP THREE

When we encode our thoughts or feelings into words, tone of voice, body language, etc., we then must decide how much of the encoding to express. Much of the encoding we give our thoughts or feelings is done subconsciously; it occurs without careful or logical thought. On the other hand, much of the expression we allow ourselves to make to others is consciously decided. We may choose to suppress the natural encoding and consciously choose a different encoding to disguise what we think or feel. We usually do that only if we fear that the other person's reaction to our thought or feeling may threaten us in some way.

When you were a kid, did you ever find yourself writing a note to the person you were sweet on instead of asking directly about his or her feelings? "Dear Jessica, I think I may like you. Do you like me? Check here for yes _____ and here for no _____." Because of fear of rejection, perhaps even ridicule, the thought and emotion express themselves in less than a clearly revealing manner.

A woman just told us on the phone that her husband of twenty-two years is one of those guys who thinks, "I told you twenty-two years ago that I loved you, and if I change my mind, I'll let you know." While we figure she is exaggerating, we understood her to be telling us that he is a man who doesn't express emotions easily. Somewhere, somehow, he was taught that he should fear that. Maybe he was rejected many times in his young life. Perhaps his father taught him—either by words or the model of his own life—that real men don't tell others what they feel. Either of those scenarios would create fear of a negative reaction if he were to openly share the emotion he felt for his wife. The first could cause him to think, "She'll reject or ridicule me if I make myself vulnerable by telling her the depth of what I feel for her." The second could make him fear, "She'll think I'm weak—not a real man—if I get all gushy with my words or actions." One thing is for sure, if he feels deep emotion for her, he isn't communicating it. That would mean his communication fails at step three, expression.

In *Becoming ONE* Joe Beam explains how many men really want to talk to their wives but are afraid that she will somehow react negatively. They fear hurting her; they cannot cope with making her cry. They really cannot deal with her withdrawing by pouting, leaving to visit Mother for a while, or giving the silent treatment. So rather than risk rejection on any level, they simply refuse to express what they really think or feel. Joe found it fascinating to find so many men who had *thought* very expressive words and *pictured* very romantic actions, but who had never spoken any of those words or done any of those actions. They were encoding what they felt, but they suppressed the expression time after time so that they very well disguised what they thought or felt.

If you feel that your wife, husband, parent(s), or children aren't sharing what they really feel, you may be right. We'll soon tell you how you may change this process.

FAILURE DURING STEP FOUR

We register the expressions of other people to us through one or more of our five senses. We see what they write. We hear what they say. If they are in our presence when they say it, we see the nonverbals accompanying their words. If they touch us, we feel the touch. Even the fragrances we smell or the kiss we taste can become part of the communication process. Obviously, the more senses we have operating correctly, the easier it should be to receive what the other person is trying to express to us.

As hearing fails, some of the effectiveness of receiving is lost. Same with eyesight or any other sense. When one or more senses decline, we attempt to balance by more effectively using our remaining senses.

The greater problems in receiving the expressions of another usually aren't in the *lack* of senses, but in the lack of *using* the senses we have. If a child tells his father about his day and the father flips on the television and keeps one eye glued to the game, he cannot clearly hear the subtleties of his child's message. No matter how well the child encodes or expresses, the dad is going to miss part of it because he isn't focused on it.

Most often when we hear a spouse say, "My husband/wife doesn't listen to me," we discover by further questioning what the speaker means. Usually he or she can't get unbroken eye contact from the spouse or get the spouse to listen without occasionally tuning out to focus on other things.

How many times in your home has a spouse, child, or parent responded inappropriately to something you said? If you expressed your thought or feeling clearly, the misinterpretation may have begun in the very act of receiving your message. When a person hears only bits and pieces, or when that person misses crucial nonverbals, he or she can't interpret the message clearly. Important ingredients needed for the interpretation never got to his or her brain.

FAILURE DURING STEP FIVE

It would be logical to think that if steps 1–4 are done well, step 5 should be very easy to do right.

Wouldn't it be great if it always turned out that way?

But we humans have ways of confusing even the simplest of tasks. We know from what has been written already that the sender could encode his or her thoughts or feelings incorrectly. The same kind of error can happen on the receiving side. Even when the sender has a clear thought, encodes it clearly, and expresses it well, the receiver may misinterpret the communication—even if the receiver focused his senses on receiving. How could that happen? In at least two ways:

1. The sender encoded with the right words, nonverbals, etc., but the receiver misunderstood the words or gestures.

2. The receiver did understand correctly the sender's code and expressions, but through a flaw of reasoning misinterpreted them anyway.

You recall that in our illustration in step 2, we mentioned that a child could mistakenly choose the wrong word and cause miscommunication between himself and his mother. The reverse could happen on the receiver's side: The child employs the correct word, but the mother mistakenly believes the word has a different meaning.

For example, a parent tells a teen to come straight home from a party. On his way home, he drops off two of his friends, which causes him to be slightly tardy in his arrival. When the parent questions where he's been, he innocently replies that it took an extra fifteen minutes to go by his friends' houses to take them home. The parent angrily complains that the teen disobeyed, and he responds in a hurt voice that he did come straight home. To him coming straight home never precluded dropping off friends; it meant not going to get a burger or checking out another party. Both parent and teen go to bed upset, mumbling about the density of the other. Was the problem with the sender? Perhaps. Was it with the receiver? Maybe. (Your view likely is based on whether you are a parent or teen!) One thing is obvious; the receiver misinterpreted the communication from the sender because his understanding of "straight home" varied from that of his parent.

The same kind of thing can happen when the receiver interprets the nonverbals incorrectly. ("But you were laughing when you said it, so I assumed you were kidding around. I didn't know you were talking to me during a commercial break from *America's Funniest Personal Injury Lawyers*.")

Even when sender and receiver understand all encodings similarly, there's always the possibility that a glitch occurs in the interpreting process. Have you ever heard everything the other person said, knew that you understood exactly what he or she was trying to communicate, only to discover in a day or so that you didn't get it at all? Every business in the world has likely experienced that in communications between employee and supervisor. Maybe every family in the world has had that occur in communications between spouses, parents, or kids. "I'm sure you said..." encounters a dull stare and a lengthy explanation of the foregoing conversation. "Yeah, that's what you said and I...oh...I guess I got that turned around in my brain somehow. I knew what you said, but it lodged in my brain's 'to do' list as something totally different. Sorry."

We'll show you how to keep this kind of miscommunication from taking place in just a few paragraphs.

FAILURE DURING STEP SIX

"Surely," you must be thinking now, "if the first five steps work well, the sixth is a given. Right?"

Wrong.

Even when we completely understand the message being communicated to us by another, we may not react to it at all. We understand the other person's intent, thought, feeling, or desire, but we choose to immediately dismiss it and move to some unrelated matter without so much as a word, gesture, or anything else.

Even the wrong reaction is better than no reaction. If the other person communicates love and we respond with anger, that at least creates an exchange. We have a place to begin, something from which to create clear communication (assuming that anger in the receiver doesn't throw the sender off track and propel him into immediate anger as well).

Several years ago we read of a mother who would punish her child by completely ignoring her. For a week or two, no communication from the child received any response at all. It was as if the mother had gone deaf, blind, and dumb in an instant and the daughter had no means with which to reach her. After several days the child would finally fall apart emotionally, mourning, begging, and pleading for her mother to acknowledge that the daughter was even alive. When the mother felt the punishment reached sufficient levels, she would finally speak. Her first words were always a warning as to how bad things would be the next time the child misbehaved.

We never saw a follow-up study on the child, but we assume the long-term effects were devastating. No one wants to witness a child and parent vehemently arguing—just as we avoid hearing any two people fighting with each other—but arguing can be guided into positive communication with wise intervention. Cutting the other person off from all communication—giving absolutely no response—can destroy the relationship entirely.

Step 6, reacting, means that the receiver communicates back to the sender. The receiver may ask for clarification. He may disagree. He may indicate approval or agreement. But as long as he or she is reacting to what the other person meant to convey, communication is taking place.

The receiver becomes the sender. He or she has a thought or feeling in response to the sender's message. He then encodes that thought or feeling and expresses it clearly. The sender obviously becomes the receiver. He or she must attune to the expression, decode it by interpreting it, and react.

As each person takes turns being the sender or receiver, real communication takes place.

How Do You Overcome Failure at Any Step?

We said earlier that even when a person doesn't have a clear thought or feeling, he or she can still communicate, and real understanding can take place. Rather than trying to encode thoughts or feelings that aren't clear, the sender encodes the thought that he or she *isn't* clear in thought or feeling.

In our example in step 1, a distraught wife wasn't sure why she was distraught and was trying to communicate with her husband. We gave a few possibilities of how that would fail if she sent a garbled message to him. To keep the message from being garbled, she could do something like the following:

Encoding her words with appropriate body language, tone of voice, etc. to communicate to him both her distress and her confused feelings about it, she could say, "I'm really upset, but there isn't any one thing I feel upset about. I feel unhappy and kind of depressed, but those words don't quite explain what's inside me. Could you help me work through this?" By doing so she is clearly communicating her distress, but at the same time she isn't asking him to react in any way other than to help her figure out why she feels it. As he listens and decodes (interprets) her message, he knows that he doesn't have to understand what is going on with her at this point. That removes pressure from the situation. He also knows that his job is to become the sender, but he isn't to be sending answers, just questions. That keeps her from feeling more dismay by the husband's moving into the role of "fixer" before she even knows what needs to be fixed. She isn't asking for a white knight to rescue her, just a friend to help her understand herself.

While this may seem very elementary, pay close attention to this point. Dr. Ron Braund, executive director of the Alpha Counseling Centers in Atlanta, Georgia, says, "It's especially important for women to understand that the first things out of a husband's mouth aren't necessarily what he's trying to communicate. I find that many men are processors. They throw an idea out and then talk it through. By the time they finish exploring it, they become sure of what they think or feel, and that might be quite different from the thing they originally said. So I tell wives all the time not to react negatively to the first thing he says, but to help him think it through."[4]

Based on what we've written above, you know that we think the husband could vastly improve the communication process if he were to tell his wife that he isn't sure of what he thinks or feels. He could create a much better communication environment, one in which the wife is much less likely to make incorrect interpretations, if he would tell her he's processing and ask her assistance in helping him do that.

The trouble with that, according to Dr. Braund, is that men themselves don't realize that's what they are doing. It's so natural for them to do that they aren't cognizant that they're doing it.

Therefore, we give the following suggestions to men and women, boys and girls.

◆ When you aren't sure of what you think or feel, tell the other person as soon as you realize it. It will keep your communication from derailing from the six steps and will lead to a wonderful conversation.

◆ If you become frustrated with a person you're talking to because you aren't quite sure where he or she is headed, ask if they are thinking this through or if they have already made up their minds. If they're thinking it through, cease reacting from a personal reference and begin reacting as a counselor or guide who helps someone evaluate a matter. You'll still need to attune and interpret, but you can do so from a more objective frame of mind.

Hear this last point well: Anytime there seems to be a flaw in any step, the receiver should calmly and unemotionally ask for clarification. "I don't think I'm understanding what you're saying," or "Do you mean…?"

◆ It's always better to ask than to assume.

◆ It's always better to clarify than to combat.

Recall the illustration earlier where the parent and teen failed to understand each other about what "come straight home" means? If the parent had run through a litany of things excluded by "come straight home," the teen likely would have felt demeaned. "Hey, I'm not three years old, you know!" In that situation the teen would have made the communication clearer if he had asked for clarification, "Okay, I understand you don't want me going any place else, but it would be okay if I dropped a couple of my buddies at their homes, right?" The teen would have retained dignity—not feeling he was being talked down to as one who couldn't reason or think—and the parent would have had a chance to clarify his intentions.

Each person, not just the sender, has a role in making sure that communication is a clear interchange of ideas.

EXERCISE 1: LEARNING HOW THE MODEL APPLIES TO YOUR FAMILY

In the six steps of the Communication Model, we gave examples of how each step could fail. We encourage you to do a fun exercise (no sensitive or embarrassing illustrations, just ones the family can laugh about now) with those six steps. List at least one example for each step where someone in your family had a less than outstanding experience with that step while trying to communicate. Jot down your memories of these events before meeting together and then, if you haven't already written it, jot down the event that the family most enjoyed remembering.

1. Sender's clear thought or feelings:

2. Accurate encoding of the thought or feeling:

3. Clear expression without withholding any encoding:

4. Receiver attuned to sender's expression:

5. Accurate interpretation of the sender's message:

6. Valid reaction:

We designed the exercises in this chapter to bring family members closer together. Be aware that as you incorporate younger family members into these exercises, they may react with resentment if the sessions are too long. Therefore, we recommend that you set a maximum time limit (appropriate for your family members' ages and temperaments) for each session. It's better to have two sessions or to slightly speed up a project to finish in a prescribed time limit than to turn these exercises into dreaded drudgery. Have fun! If everyone is enjoying themselves, let a session run longer. Remember, these exercises are made for your family, not your family for these exercises!

EXERCISE 2:
HANDLING CONFLICT

In *Fantastic Families* we suggest that no family member should approach conflict with a win/lose attitude. If one person wants to get his or her way, even to the detriment of one or more family members, conflict isn't being handled as it should. The ideal is compromise or consensus—"Let's find a way that everyone can have victory."

In *Fantastic Families* we give six tactics for reaching compromise or consensus:

Tactic #1—Deal with conflicts quickly. The longer you wait, the greater the difficulty in solving it.

Tactic #2—Deal with one issue at a time. "How do you eat an elephant? One bite at the time."

Tactic #3—Be specific. Generalities fix nothing. What is the specific problem? What is a specific solution we can all accept?

Tactic #4—Become allies. Picture yourselves as being on the same side of the table trying to find the best solution, not opposing sides of the table at war.

Tactic #5—Ban the bombs. No one wants to compromise when he or she feels attacked.

Tactic #6—Open up understanding. The more we know of each other's perspective, the better we can solve the problem.

We offer you a methodology for applying those six tactics. In Family Dynamics's *Negotiating Marriage* seminar,[5] we teach married couples how to solve conflicts by a method that makes both spouses happy. While we can't give the details here, we do in that seminar. We believe this succinct overview will help you use these methods with your family.

- ◆ You must know what the conflict is about on a core level.

- ◆ Agree that no solution will be implemented until all parties enthusiastically agree.

- ◆ Do a self-examination to understand on an emotional level why you feel about it the way you do.

- ◆ Listen carefully to the other person as he or she explains what he or she feels and why.

- ◆ Brainstorm with abandon until an agreeable solution is found.

- ◆ Apply the solution when all parties enthusiastically agree, and evaluate it to see if the compromise satisfies all parties.

Now for the exercise. A parent should pick something that there is likely to be disagreement about among family members, but it must be something that is relatively unimportant to everyone. (In our *Negotiating Marriage* seminar, we recommend they imagine a visit to the grocery store. Each person gets to pick food items to purchase. The catch is that no one can buy anything unless everyone enthusiastically agrees. As soon as you discover a food there is disagreement about, start the problem solving process. If you use this for your exercise, note that it may be a better learning experience if more than one family member wants the item and more than one family member refuses to agree.)

Once you've found something you would disagree about, every person speaks—using the Communication Model—while everyone else listens. The goal is for every person to answer the following questions and for every other family member to clearly understand the answers. Have each family member answer question 1 until the parent in charge is satisfied that the family is ready for question 2. Move to question 3 only when you're sure everyone has completely answered question 2. The process continues in that fashion until the conflict is resolved. As you work through this exercise, make notes of what *you* think and what *others* say.

1.   What is the specific conflict?

2.   Why does each person feel about the conflict the way that he or she does? (Why do you want this certain thing? Think deeply and explore your feelings. Why do you not want this? Think deeply as to why you are opposed to this. Help each person who speaks explore his thoughts or feelings rather than reacting positively or negatively to those feelings.)

3.   Each person gives a synopsis of what each other person feels and why they feel that way. (Be sure to ask each person if the speaker correctly represented his or her thoughts or feelings. If not, then have the person clarify to the speaker until the speaker can verbalize the person's thoughts or feelings to the person's satisfaction.)

4. When it is clear that everyone understands everyone else, open the floor for a brainstorming session that offers possible solutions that could make everyone happy. (Make it clear that in brainstorming there are no evaluations of any suggestion. One is as good as another, and none should be argued against, ridiculed, rejected, etc.)

5. After all potential solutions have been offered, have a group discussion until you find one with which everyone enthusiastically agrees.

6. Since this is an imaginary problem, ask each person to describe how well he or she thinks the compromised solution would work.

When conflict next arises in your family, have the members in conflict work through these same six questions. Make sure to apply the compromise and don't be afraid to revisit the questions if the attempted solution fails to satisfy everyone. Rather than starting again with number 1, start with number 5. If the members in conflict easily agree on another alternative already listed by the previous brainstorming session, implement it. If they cannot find a mutually agreeable solution, move back to number 4 and brainstorm again. If that isn't helping, move to number 3 and so on until you find the right starting place. Then start back down the numbers again until you find a solution to attempt.

 FAMILY AT WORK   *Putting It to Work—Six Ideas for Your Family*

In *Fantastic Families* we offer six ideas for your family.
1. Set aside time each day to talk with each other. (The book specifically mentions spouses talking with each other. We expand it here to the entire family's talking with each other.)
2. Take an objective look at your communication habits.

3. Designate a mealtime as a time for sharing.
4. Establish rituals and traditions.
5. Keep a family diary or journal.
6. On birthdays, videotape the birthday child.

As we do in every chapter, we ask that you pick at least one of the ideas for your family to begin implementing this week. Because of the similar nature of the suggestions, we combine these six ideas into two potential activities for your family to choose.

1. COMBINE IDEAS 1, 2, AND 3

If you choose this activity, have the family agree on a time every week when there will just be sharing. Don't combine this with family meetings because those always deal with business. This should be a relaxed time during which each person can share his or her day, life, feelings, hopes, wishes, creative thoughts, or anything else. You may make it a specific meal every day, such as dinner. You may choose to make it a special time during the week, like visiting over ice cream on Sunday evenings. The important thing is that every person in the family knows when it is going to occur and sacrifices other activities to be present. (Yes, parent[s], this applies to you too.)

Sharing time is ideal for taking an objective look at your communication habits. Write the six steps from the Communication Model on index cards and give a copy to each family member.[6]

As each person shares, other family members casually evaluate how well the interchange of ideas is going. They use their index card to remind them how to listen, to discover when someone isn't really listening, and to ask questions about words, gestures, tone of voice, etc. that don't clearly communicate to them. Their index cards should help them know when to move into the role of counselor rather than a listener. As each person becomes conscious of the model, we predict communication between family members will improve in quality and quantity.

2. COMBINE IDEAS 4, 5, AND 6

If your family chooses to establish rituals and traditions that will promote communication, the two ideas listed above as suggestions five and six make good traditions.

If you choose the diary or journal, designate who will be the scribe, how often the entries will be read to the entire family, and how other family members can make approval or amendments.

If you choose making a video of each person on his or her birthday, plan how you will do the video. For example, in addition to candid shots of cake, ice cream, party, and the like, you may want to interview the birthday person with specific questions. The whole family could agree on the questions, and every year the birthday person would answer the "birthday interview" questions. You could ask things like:

- What was the best thing that happened to you in the last year?

- How have you changed most since your last birthday?

- What plans do you have for your future? (This question would work well even if the answer is the same every year. Grown children may look at these later in life and note that they "always wanted to be..." That could be either a great satisfaction or a great motivator.

- How would you describe your relationship with God?

- Who is your love interest right now?

- Twenty years from now, what is the one thing you would like to remember about your life as it is now?

We're sure that with your creativity your family can develop some very wonderful and touching questions.

Another dimension to this ritual could be to interview every other family member with one question: "What would you personally want the birthday person to know that you felt on this day?"

If you ended each person's birthday watching randomly picked birthday videos of every family member, birthdays might become the best days of your family's year.

HELPING OTHERS

If as a parent or older child you volunteered to help younger children during this lesson, you likely will find information below that will help you decide how to adapt material in this chapter to specific age groups.

For example, you note from the following chart that teaching a child in the kindergarten–grade 3 age span could involve asking a lot of questions to help the child learn self-expression. But just as important would be to help the child learn listening skills. That might be as simple as asking the child to be quiet and listen. It could be as interesting as playing a game where the child has to be able to tell you certain things that he or she could only know by listening carefully as you speak. For more mature children in that age group, you could add the dimension to that game of using gestures or facial expressions and asking the child what he or she thinks they mean.

For the age group that includes preschool–kindergarten, word games (on their level, naturally) would be a good way to begin to teach valid communication skills.

We trust that your judgment and creativity will lead you to effective ways to include the family member you've volunteered to help.

A LAST WORD OF ENCOURAGEMENT

As we end this chapter, we realize that it may have taken more effort from your family because of its length and intensity. We feel that this chapter is one of the most important in this workbook and sincerely hope that your family has taken the time to read and apply all that's in it.

Nick Stinnett's research has convinced him that of the six characteristics of strong families, commitment is the most important. Joe Beam agrees completely but adds this statement: "Once you know that every family member is committed to making the family strong, you then have to learn to understand each other and fulfill each person's needs. The only way we know to make that happen is clear communication. Master that, and you're well on your way to building all the other characteristics into your family."

The next chapter takes us into another powerful characteristic of a strong family—spending time together.

Communication

- ◆ Expressing feelings of support, love, affection
- ◆ Building communication skills, including listening
- ◆ Establishing emotional intimacy
- ◆ Sharing information through teaching

Prenatal/Birth	Infancy
Sharing information	Bonding/physical contact
	One-to-one interaction
	Sensory discrimination, hand-eye coordination
	Freedom of movement
	Language development through supportive responses
	Soothing language

Preschool–Kindergarten	Kindergarten–Grade 3
Enjoying music, poetry, art, and games	Developing social skills/manners
Self-regulation	Communicating with others, listening
Developing autonomy	Communicating affection to family members
Prosocial behaviors	Using memory, vocabulary, and imagination
Self-discovery	
Shared language activities	

Grades 4–5	Grades 6–8
Making and keeping friends	Encouraging family/school communication
Building communication skills	Negotiating family rules

Getting along with parents	Sharing and keeping confidences
Following directions	Functioning as a teacher to other family members

Grades 9–12	**Early Adult**
Active listening/public speaking	Realizing gender differences in interpersonal relationships
Communicating love and affection	Developing communication skills for professional development and growth
Self-disclosure	Developing communication skills with family members and other age groups
Communicating a positive self-image	Developing responsiveness
Making responsible sexual decisions	
Resolving conflict	

Middle Adult	**Later Adult**
Building partnerships and contractual agreements	Lessened ability to see/hear compensation for loss
Redefining values	Accepting and expressing feelings and needs
Nurturing	Changes in patterns of friendships
Linking family to community and institutions	Dealing with a new environment
Articulating family changing roles	Strengthening extended families
Marriage adjustment	Planning for the future/retirement
	Communicating optimism

STEP FOUR
SPEND TIME TOGETHER

Although he's made myriad presentations around the world, Joe Beam felt slightly uneasy as he walked into the foyer of Mount Pleasant Christian Church. He figured the bright spot of the evening would be meeting John and Janet Milenbaugh, a very special couple among the thousands certified by Family Dynamics to lead its interactive courses. Because of the Milenbaughs' outstanding results with Family Dynamics's *His Needs, Her Needs* course, Mount Pleasant had booked and heavily advertised the special *Love, Sex & Marriage* weekend. Joe's uneasiness stemmed from the fact that since the church had booked the seminar "sight unseen," they might be surprised by its candor. Every church that sponsors LSM gives it great reviews ("No one has *ever* dealt with those crucial subjects as straightforwardly as that!"), but Joe always worries that each new sponsoring church might view it differently. As he entered Mount Pleasant, he knew he would be apprehensive until he met the ministers and gauged their ability to honestly address family matters.

It didn't take long to find out.

Reggie Epps, senior minister at Mount Pleasant, introduced himself with a few warm words and then looked Joe right in the eye. "My wife and I won't be here for tomorrow's session. I know there are several good reasons I should be here, but my daughter has a basketball game, and I'll be there. It wouldn't matter if you died and needed me to do the funeral, I'd be at that game."

No beating around the bush with Reggie. He knew what was important and wasted no words in explaining to Joe that nothing he could say or do would change the situation. He was nice, polite, and friendly, but he made his point firmly.

Joe liked Reggie immediately. He also lost his anxiety about the seminar's being received well at that church. When the senior minister has that much awareness of what's important to his family and is that frank in making it known, Joe had nothing to worry about in being candid himself.

We wish that everyone had the same sense of family responsibility that Reggie and his wife have—a deep seated commitment to spend the time to make wonderful family memories.

Many years ago a woman in her thirties cried bitterly as she told us how throughout her childhood her father never attended any of her athletic contests. "He never missed my brother's games. He never made one of mine. Can you imagine how I felt? How I feel now, all these years later? I spent my childhood finding one thing after another to excel in just hoping that my father would notice and want to be around me. I never found it. Never. He never had time for me, no matter what I did."

Wouldn't it be terrible to hear that from any child years after they've left your home?

Wouldn't it hurt to hear a brother or sister someday say, "I never learned who you are, and it's a given that you don't really know me. We grew up in the same house but never, never did anything together or had anything in common. We're strangers with the same bloodline. Strangers, little more."

Those aren't imaginary words in the paragraphs above. We've heard all of them uttered by at least one disenfranchised person, either to us or to family members in counseling sessions. Hurt that never should have happened did happen because of the misuse of one of life's most precious gifts—time.

Time is a commodity that can never be reused, rewound, or replaced. It advances at an unyielding pace, with neither hesitation nor heed to our pleadings that it turn back on itself so that we may undo what we have done.

Or do what we have left undone.

We're not encouraging families to stifle each other by constantly being underfoot. In *Fantastic Families* we make that point clear. But we are urging every person in every family to make time to share with each other. Most friends from school—elementary through college—finally fade into casual memories as years pass. Family should be forever.

◆ ◆ ◆

EXERCISE 1:
TAKING RESPONSIBILITY

All too often modern families find themselves time-bankrupt. So much work, so many responsibilities, so much to do. We've let that become the norm in our society.

It's a sure bet that when parents let that happen in their lives, they teach their children to do the same. Home evolves from a warm family focal point to a bustling transition hub. Rather than the idyllic scenes depicted by grand masters, it more nearly resembles Grand Central Station during rush hour. The entire family may seldom be in the same room, and when they are, someone is in a hurry to be someplace else.

Counselors and therapists deal with the consequences of time-deprived family members. Loneliness. Loss of identity. Isolation. Depression. Anxiety. Alienation. Vulnerability to extramarital affairs, unplanned pregnancies, drug abuse. No, not all these definitely happen, but many people in families who don't have time for them suffer one or more of these aftereffects.

Whose responsibility is it to change this? Who should ensure that the family spends time together?

Not the kids. Even though it's nearly a sure thing that younger children will beg for it, demand it when they think they can. They instinctively know they need love demonstrated copiously in both quality and quantity. An hour or two of "quality time" in a week doesn't begin to fulfill their cravings for attention and caring. Neither will twenty hours of sitting in the same room with a parent or parents who are focused on television, reading, or napping on the sofa.

The responsibility lies squarely on the shoulders of the parent(s). If older children live in the home—older teens—they're probably going to share in that responsibility. Any negatives they learned from their parent(s) about time usage may be more quickly reoriented by helping the parent(s) change the family's pattern. In other words, they likely will do much better in altering their patterns by getting to help define what needs to change and how it should change than by being told what changes they will have to adjust to.

So, parent(s) and, if applicable, older teens, answer these questions as you think through them together. As you answer, keep Webster's definition of *quality* in mind: "an essential or distinctive characteristic, property, or attribute...character with respect to fineness, or grade of excellence... high grade; superiority; excellence."[1] Webster goes on to define *quality time* as "time devoted exclusively to nurturing a cherished person or activity."

1. What definition and descriptions can we give for quality time so that we will know when our family is experiencing it?

2. How much time in an average week do we actually spend as a family that we could *honestly* call quality time by our definition above?

3.   How is each individual in the family affected by our average amount of quality time? Who needs more? Why?

4.   How much quality time will we *commit* to spend with the family in an average week?

5.   What changes do we need to make in our thinking if we are to rearrange our lives to create more quality time?

6.   How can we help each other make this happen?

We designed the exercises in this chapter to bring family members closer together. Be aware that as you incorporate younger family members into these exercises, they may react with resentment if the sessions are too long. Therefore, we recommend that you set a maximum time limit (appropriate for your family members' ages and temperaments) for each session. It's better to have two sessions or to slightly speed up a project to finish in a prescribed time limit than to turn these exercises into dreaded drudgery. Have fun! If everyone is enjoying themselves, let a session run longer. Remember, these exercises are made for your family, not your family for these exercises!

◆ ◆ ◆

EXERCISE 2: SIX SUGGESTIONS FOR QUALITY TIME

In *Fantastic Families* we present six suggestions for spending more quality time together as a family.

Suggestion #1—Share meals together

Suggestion #2—Do house and yard chores together

Suggestion #3—Play together

Suggestion #4—Enjoy religious, club, and school activities together

Suggestion #5—Spend special events together

Suggestion #6—Do nothing in particular

In this exercise, we ask the parent(s) to poll the entire family during a family meeting to see which of the six suggestions the family would like to implement. Since these are to be ongoing activities, make sure that they are doable over time—in other words, your schedule can be altered permanently to do them— and that all family members commit to the activity. Feel free to implement more than one. Do them all if you wish. Just make sure that at least one of them is on a regular schedule, either daily or weekly. Others may be seasonal or occasional.

1. SHARE MEALS TOGETHER

Many families make a commitment to being present for a specific meal *every* day. For some that means breakfast: "Okay. Okay. I'll get up!" For others it means dinner: "I'll leave whatever is pressing at work and come home to my family."

If you choose this option, you may want to include weekly coupons that can be cashed in by family members. That means that each family member could use one coupon each week to miss the designated meal. If Dad just *had* to work late one night, he could call before dinner and cash in his coupon. If Sis just *has* to be at cheerleading tryouts, she could cash in her coupon the day before so that everyone knows where she is during dinner of the excused day. If you use this system, we recommend that you hold all family members to one coupon per week and that you allow all the family to share their views about whether they thought the coupon was wisely used. At the next meal when all are present, list coupons used that week and let the family say what they think. Be sure to allow the person who used the coupon to give his or her reasoning as to why using the coupon was valid. (The results of these conversations may occasionally mean that coupons may be disallowed for certain situations. "No more cashing in coupons to go see your girlfriend an hour early.") We also recommend that you set a limit on how many family members may use coupons on any one day. "Sorry, but a coupon for Tuesday has already been cashed. You'll have to be here."

2. DO HOUSE AND YARD CHORES TOGETHER

From shoveling snow to raking leaves to trimming the hedges, there are many things families may do outdoors that would be productive and create an opportunity to interact. Obviously the person running the lawn mower can't be involved in conversation, but many other activities, like raking, could easily be done by two family members at a time. As they rake, pile, bag, or burn, they can talk about everything from the task at hand to what they want for their birthdays.

The same thing goes for indoor tasks. Don't just have one person folding clothes from the dryer. Have at least two. Maybe even three. The more the merrier! Encourage conversation as they work. If they don't know what to talk about, have them sing together. Remember, the primary object isn't getting the task done (although that helps the family); it's getting each family member to spend quality time with other family members.

3. PLAY TOGETHER

Walk into any sporting goods, toy, or discount store and check out the games for families. There are several that cross lines of age and maturity. Even a toddler can play croquet or Putt-Putt. Though no one expects her to win, she can still have an enjoyable time with the rest of the family. The Beams used to have two sizes of basketballs so that all three daughters (spaced over 19 years) could play "horse" with Dad at the same time.

Some games, of course, are more specialized. That's fine too. Have a game night where each is involved in some game with at least one other family member.

4. ENJOY RELIGIOUS, CLUB, AND SCHOOL ACTIVITIES TOGETHER

We don't mean to equate a family's religion with their social activities, but all these afford opportunity for time together. Because one of the six characteristics of strong families is spiritual well-being, we especially urge you to consider family religious activities. Attending religious services and activities as a family does more than just give you time together, it strengthens spiritual bonds between family members.

If your child has an opportunity to be involved in extracurricular activities at school, clear out time in the schedule of at least one parent (sometimes this can be an older teen) and be there for the event. Alice Beam spent a day (*and a night* on the *cold hard floor!*) during an educational zoo trip with ten-year-old Kimberly and classmates from her gifted children's class. When daughter Joanna was fourteen, Joe Beam flew her to Seattle with him so she could attend a weekend youth rally on Whidbey Island where Joe was speaking. Although both events called for sacrifices on the parts of each parent (Joanna wanted to fly first class!), each of the daughters will remember for a lifetime the special time they spent with a parent.

Attending these events together takes much more effort on the part of the parent than the child. As your family considers this option, we remind the parent(s) and older teens of the commitments they made in exercise 1 in this chapter.

5. SPEND SPECIAL EVENTS TOGETHER

When Reggie and Shara Epps sacrificed a church event that would have been a valuable experience for them and instead attended the ballgame of their daughter, they did a wonderful thing. How many times does a daughter get to play in a semifinal game? How much more special is that game when both parents are there to cheer her on?

Many special events take place in life. As we get older, the value of previous events diminish in memory. When we graduate from college, we likely won't compare it to our graduation from kindergarten. We may not even remember that day. But the effect our parents made on our lives by being there and making us feel so very special and important plays a part in everything we have done since, including college graduation. We may not remember every event, but we feel the effect of our parents' being there for us. We know we are loved, appreciated, and admired. We know we're special and can make a special life. We know this because our parents did more than tell us we were special; they showed us at every event we considered important at that stage of our lives.

6. DO NOTHING IN PARTICULAR

Sometimes the best time one can have with another person is to just be together doing nothing in particular. True friends experience this. Ever have a conversation like this with your best pal when you were a kid?

"Whadaya wanna do?"

"I dunno. Nuttin, I guess. You?"

"I duncare. You ready?"

"Yeah. Les go."

That's why you were best pals. You were comfortable just being together and seeing what life turned up next.

The same thing can happen in a family. An impromptu weekend erupts when everyone throws a few things together and piles into the car with no distinct destination. A walk around the block that started with someone noticing Mom lacing her walking shoes ends up with the whole family, including the dog, laughing through a two-mile jaunt. Lying around the patio or pool just talking, singing, or telling jokes together. Nothing special, just having fun being together. Hard to plan, but wonderful to experience when it happens.

TAKE A VOTE

As we suggested earlier, the family should discuss these suggestions and decide which activities you will do together and any ground rules you wish to apply. Talk it over and write your family decision(s) here. Write as many as you wish.

1. We decided that we will do _____ on this schedule and with these ground rules:

2. We decided that we will do _____ on this schedule and with these ground rules:

3. We decided that we will do _____ on this schedule and with these ground rules:

4. We decided that we will do _____ on
this schedule and with these ground rules:

5. We decided that we will do _____ on
this schedule and with these ground rules:

6. We decided that we will do _____ on
this schedule and with these ground rules:

FAMILY AT WORK

Putting It to Work—Six Ideas for Your Family

We admit that we made exercise 2 much in the same way we've done "Putting It to Work" in previous chapters. The difference is that we've requested in every chapter that you must at least begin, if not complete, the chosen activity from exercise 3 during the week. We've given you the liberty of making your own schedule for the activity or activities you choose in exercise 2 above.

Since we've changed the format of exercise 2 in this chapter, we also change the format of "Putting It to Work." We give you each of the six ideas from *Fantastic Families*, but rather than letting you choose, we assign the one you do this week. You may do more, of course, but the one we assign is special and should be done first. If you are enrolled in a *Fantastic Families* course, you will have a special class activity based on this assignment.

These are the six ideas from *Fantastic Families*:

1. Take a journey of happy memories.

2. Set aside fifteen minutes when the kids come in from school to share a snack and talk.
3. Designate one wall (or room) for family mementos.
4. Work together to design a family crest, symbol, or logo.
5. Write down or tape-record your family's history.
6. Plan opportunities for one-on-one relationships to grow.

MAKING A FAMILY CREST

The specific exercise we assign is number 4, work together to design a family crest, added in this workbook. If you prefer a logo or symbol, please complete all the steps of this exercise until instructed differently. We insert a note of caution if you choose creating a logo or symbol rather than a crest. Creating the crest calls for joint family participation from beginning to end. Creating a logo or symbol requires individuals to employ their own creativity. We think it may be too difficult for the family to try to come up with an agreeable creation while meeting together. There must be time for ideas to germinate as well as plenty of time for trial and error.

When individuals bring their creations to the group, you may experience some family members' feeling rejected if their logo or symbol isn't chosen. If you think your family is mature enough to handle that, proceed with that option. If not, we strongly suggest you create a crest instead.

It may be that someone in your family researched and already found a family crest that has existed through the years. That's wonderful, but the task we assign isn't to copy that one, or to display that one. We ask that you spend time together as a family answering the following questions and then designing your crest (logo, symbol) based on your answers.

1. What one word most clearly represents what your family is like? (This could be a word like strong, funny, brave, spiritual, outgoing, private, analytical, etc. Discuss this until members agree on the word that best describes the family.)

2. What phrase most clearly expresses the family's strongest motivation? (This might be a phrase like "We stick together," or "We love God on high," or "We look to the future instead of to the past," or "We think things through," etc. As you discuss this, don't let any one family member impose his or her phrase. Make sure that members agree that the phrase you choose best describes the predominant motivation that drives family decisions and goals.)

3. What is the most important goal jointly held by all family members? (This could be a goal like "We will be in heaven together," or "We will prepare each other to face the world," or "We will always provide a safe haven for any of us who need it," or "We will each make a difference during our lives," etc. Again, don't let any one person dominate. Seek to find the most important goal—whatever it is— shared by the whole family.)

4. Read again your answer to question 1. What object best represents the word you chose? (It can be an animal, icon, historical person, machine, plant, etc. The only limitation is that it must be something that can be drawn or photographed.)

5. Read again your answer to question 2. What object best represents the phrase you chose? (It can be an animal, icon, historical person, machine, plant, etc. The only limitation is that it must be something that can be drawn or photographed.)

6. Read again your answer to question 3. What object best represents the goal you chose? (It can be an animal, icon, historical person, machine, plant, etc. The only limitation is that it must be something that can be drawn or photographed.)

Because you answered each of the six questions above, you have one word, two phrases, and three objects. To design a crest, the next step is to choose the wording to go on your crest. Have the family talk about which they would want on the crest—the descriptive word, the motivation phrase, or the goal phrase. When you feel that you've discussed it enough to come to a conclusion, ask the family to vote. If the vote doesn't make the choice decidedly clear, continue discussing until compromise can be reached.

You now have the wording for your crest.

The crest will also contain three symbols or pictures. They are the answers your family agreed upon for questions 4–6. If there is a very artistic person in the family, it may be a good idea to assign to him or her the task of designing the crest using the wording and objects the family agreed on. Allow each person a chance to say how he or she envisions the crest, and then put the artist to work with a stated deadline for completion.

If no one in the family is particularly artistic, you have three options.

- ◆ Option 1: Put a large sheet of paper (at least legal size, preferably much larger) on a table and have everyone sit around the table. Have one person do the drawing/layout as the family discusses what should go where, including lines that separate different parts of the crest.

- ◆ Option 2: Make good notes about why your family chose the objects you did and why you chose the wording. Take those notes to an artistic friend and ask him or her to make you a family crest based on those notes.

- ◆ Option 3: Combine options 1 and 2. Once your family has sketched a rough draft, take the draft and your notes to an artistic friend who would make a "more professional" version for you.

Make sure that your artist friend gives you all rights to the finished product. You may find that you like it so much that you have it printed on family stationery or embroidered on shirts, etc.

While we assign this as a special task to cause families to spend special time together this week, we in no way imply that the other six ideas are less important. In the future, you may wish to do one or all of them.

MAKING THE LOGO OR SYMBOL

If your family chose to create a logo or symbol rather than a crest, the next step after answering questions 1–6 is for each member to create a drawing that he or she thinks best sums up the answers to questions 1–3. Perhaps a person may choose one of the items from questions 4–6 and draw that in a unique way. More creative types may wish to draw something that has never existed before. Wordsmiths may find a way to create a special word, a unique spelling of an existing word, or a unique presentation of a word or specific letters. For ideas, family members may want to skim through magazines, newspapers, or Web sites to review common logos such as IBM's special presentation of those three letters, AT&T's unique sphere, or the special way that Coca-Cola presents the word *coke*.

When everyone has finished, the family comes back together and votes on the symbol or logo that they wish to use for the family.

HELPING OTHERS

Use the following chart to involve every member of the family in the chosen activities.

In preparing to help younger children participate in this week's activities, note that the ability for kindergarten–grade 3, "learning about work," and the ability for grades 4–5, "working cooperatively with peers," could both fit into the "chores" activity listed in suggestion #2.

The preschool–kindergarten ability, "developing school readiness through age-appropriate activities/toys," with a little creativity can be integrated into the play activity mentioned in suggestion #3.

We feel sure that by now you don't need us to give a great number of examples; you've already learned how to use the chart to find ways to include all family members—even grandparents—into the activities for each week.

In the next chapter we move to another crucial strength for strong families— spiritual wellness.

Time Together	
◆ Balancing quality/quantity time ◆ Sharing leisure, fun, humor ◆ Helping others through teaching, role modeling ◆ Recognizing individual and family needs	

Prenatal/Birth	Infancy
Birthing/parenting education	Cuddling
	Spontaneous play
	Cognition through developmentally appropriate activities/toys
	Repetitive behavior

Preschool–Kindergarten	Kindergarten–Grade 3
Expressing affection	Sharing household routines
Structured play	Learning about work
Family reading	Free play
Developing school readiness through age appropriate activities/toys	Learning through concrete activities and experiences

Grades 4–5	Grades 6–8
Developing study routines	Initiating family-fun activities
Working cooperatively with peers	Acting with consideration
Topics for mealtime sharing	Organizing family chores
Family fun/outings	Gaining individual rights and privileges
Modeling positive roles	
Learning about family members	

Grades 9–12	Early Adult
Prioritizing personal/family time	Balancing professional and private time
Sharing school/group activities	Establishing a mentor relationship
Planning cooperatively for a career	Understanding family life cycle
Growing in self-reliance	
Supporting family members	

Middle Adult	Later Adult
Balancing family and work	Invitations to family and others
Prioritizing family activities	Planning for time together
Sharing family fun and interests	Family reunions
Playing together	Celebrating family events
Volunteering in community	Overcoming compulsion to work
	Respecting time of others

STEP FIVE
NURTURE
SPIRITUAL WELL-BEING

How can people reach the deeper levels of intimacy? What should they do when they've done everything they know but still seem to be lacking something in their relationship?

The eminent researcher Dr. John Gottman, codirector of the Seattle Marital and Family Institute and professor of psychology at the University of Washington, arrived at the same answers as we did to those questions. In his bestseller, *The Seven Principles for Making Marriage Work*, he writes:

> If your marriage adheres to my first six principles, there's a good chance that your relationship is stable and happy. But if you find yourself asking, "Is that all there is?"...what may be missing is a deeper sense of shared meaning. Marriage isn't just about raising kids, splitting chores, and making love. It can also have a spiritual dimension that has to do with creating an inner life together—a culture rich with symbols and rituals, and an appreciation for your roles and goals that link you, that lead you to understand what it means to be part of the family you have become....The more you can agree about the fundamentals in life, the richer, more meaningful, and in a sense easier your marriage is likely to be.[1]

While Dr. Gottman speaks specifically to marriage, his words are just as applicable to the entire family. Good, solid relationships enter a different dimension when they find common meaning through shared spirituality. Whether husband and wife or parent and child, the deeper levels of understanding and intimacy occur with the development of shared spirituality. Barriers, walls, and defenses tend to disappear. Hope, faith, optimism, and unity take their place.

In *Fantastic Families* we point out that when you build your family on a spiritual foundation, you receive at least six blessings:

Blessing #1—Purpose or meaning

Blessing #2—Guidelines for living

Blessing #3—Freedom and peace

Blessing #4—A positive, confident outlook

Blessing #5—Support from like-minded people

Blessing #6—Access to the power of God

When a family develops spiritual well-being, the challenges of life no longer seem so overwhelming when they suddenly make themselves known. With a relationship to God that gives purpose and lasting meaning, families can look beyond present crises with hope and determination. While there will come the inevitable pains, disappointments, and separations, none of them create lasting despair. Families with spiritual well-being know that nothing that happens here is the finality of the matter. They look to the future, both in this life and the life to come. They endure because of an abiding belief that God reigns and is sovereign. While they don't always understand his actions in allowing dreaded things to occur, they trust his wisdom and look for the blessings to follow.

If you wish to have direction that unites rather than meaninglessness that alienates, you must pursue spiritual well-being with all your heart, mind, and soul.

◆ ◆ ◆

EXERCISE 1: EVERYTHING STARTS WITH THE ADULTS IN THE FAMILY

As the leader(s) of your family, you should never expect your children to reach a higher level of spiritual well-being than you. They may. But you cannot expect it. Your role is not only to encourage spiritual well-being in your children but to first model it in yourself. Parents through the ages have learned that our children are much more influenced by how we live than by what we teach. Remember the old adage: "I can't hear what you say because what you are thunders so loudly in my ears." That's the old way of saying, "If you're gonna talk the talk, you gotta walk the walk."

However you phrase it, your kids believe it.

You should too.

This exercise can be rather time consuming if you choose to do it all. Use discretion about what to complete during this week and what to complete later. We give two parts to this exercise, both aimed primarily at parents. The first one applies to all parents, single or married. (If you wish, you may have children who are mature enough to understand the questions complete the exercise as well.) The second part applies only to parents who currently have a mate.

PART ONE: AN INVENTORY
OF YOUR RELATIONSHIP WITH GOD

There are no right or wrong answers to the following survey. To get the best result, you must give your rating for all the questions with absolute honesty. We're not trying to give God insight into you; we're hoping to give you insight into yourself. You can accomplish that if you look deep within yourself and rate each statement as forthrightly as you can.

THE QUESTIONS

Rate the following statements using a 1 to 9 scale where 1 means "not at all," 5 means "moderately," and 9 means "extremely." Use the two forms supplied on the following page to write your ratings.

1	2	3	4	5	6	7	8	9
not at all				moderately				extremely

1. I feel close to God.

2. I can count on God in times of need.

3. I regularly share deeply personal information about my actions and my feelings as I pray.

4. I feel that I can really trust God.

5. I have a warm relationship with God.

6. I adore God.

7. I can't imagine anything or anyone in life making me as happy as my relationship with God does.

8. I find myself thinking about God frequently.

9. I cannot imagine a life without a relationship with God.

10. I feel passionate about my relationship with God.

11. I view my commitment to God as permanent.

12. I could not let anything or anyone get in the way of my commitment to God.

13. I have confidence in the stability of my relationship with God.

14. Even when I'm disappointed or upset about something God allowed to happen, I remain committed to our relationship.

15. I am certain of my love for God.

Rating What You Feel Is Characteristic

Rate the statements above as to how characteristic they are of your relationship with God. In other words, to what extent does each statement reflect how you currently feel? Write your answers using the 1 to 9 scale here in this form. Note that your rating for question 1 goes in block 1, rating for question 2 in block 2, and so on.

1.	6.	11.
2.	7.	12.
3.	8.	13.
4.	9.	14.
5.	10.	15.
Total Column	Total Column	Total Column
Average	Average	Average

Rating What You Think Is Important

Now rate the statements as to how important they are to your relationship with God. In other words, to what extent do you feel it is important that you should feel this way, regardless of how you actually feel? Write your answers using the 1 to 9 scale here in this form.

1.	6.	11.
2.	7.	12.
3.	8.	13.
4.	9.	14.
5.	10.	15.
Total Column	Total Column	Total Column
Average	Average	Average

UNDERSTANDING YOUR SCORES

As you may have guessed from the answer forms, at the bottom of each column you should total the score in *that* column and divide by 5 to get your average rating for that column. The first column (the one on your left) gives a brief glimpse into the intimacy you feel in your relationship with God. *By that we mean how close, connected, and bonded you feel to him.* The middle column provides a glimpse into the passion you feel in your relationship. *By that we mean how intense your feelings for God are and how much you desire him in your life.* The third column does the same for the commitment you feel for God. *By that we mean your level of decisiveness to remain in relationship with him.*

We chose these three areas—intimacy, passion, commitment—because according to the research of Dr. Sternberg at Yale, these are the three basic components of love.[2]

While we do not claim that these ratings are statistically valid or that they provide ironclad insights, we do believe they provide you a quick picture of your relationships.

Jot your averages here:

Characteristic   Importance

_____ intimacy average   _____ intimacy average

_____ passion average   _____ passion average

_____ commitment average   _____ commitment average

The first insight this exercise may give you is to compare the scores above. If your averages in the Characteristic column vary significantly from the Importance column, you see clearly that the relationship you feel you should have with God isn't the relationship you have now. If that's the case, you should answer the following two questions.

1. Which of the three is the weakest emotion you feel for God—intimacy, passion, commitment—and why is that the weakest one?

2. What do you commit to do to change your relationship with God from what it is to what you think it should be?

You can gain a second insight by asking your children (the ones who are mature enough to understand the statements) to rate you on each of the above statements. Ask them to rate you on what they perceive is characteristic of you. We realize that they cannot really know what you feel. But our goal isn't to discover if they know what you feel. The purpose of having them do this is to discover what they *perceive* that you feel. The object isn't to get an accurate score of your relationship with God, but an assessment of how they view your spiritual life.

If you ask any of your children to do this, do NOT demonstrate any negative reactions to their answers or explanations. Don't disagree with them, explain yourself, or do anything else that might communicate that you don't fully accept their answers. If you think you will not be self-controlled if you happen to hear what you don't want to hear, don't involve your children at all. You can't increase spirituality in your home by making your children wish they hadn't told you the truth!

Once the kids have rated you in terms of characteristics, have them rate the statements again in terms of importance. When they're done, jot their averages here.

Child _____

Characteristic		Importance	
_____	intimacy average	_____	intimacy average
_____	passion average	_____	passion average
_____	commitment average	_____	commitment average

Child _____

Characteristic		Importance	
_____	intimacy average	_____	intimacy average
_____	passion average	_____	passion average
_____	commitment average	_____	commitment average

Child _____

Characteristic		Importance	
_____	intimacy average	_____	intimacy average
_____	passion average	_____	passion average
_____	commitment average	_____	commitment average

Their answers may give you a clearer picture of how they perceive your spirituality. If you don't like the scores, answer these two questions.

1. What is the area where your children perceive you to be weakest in your relationship with God—intimacy, passion, commitment—and why do you think they perceive that?

2. What will you do in your everyday life that will improve your children's perceptions of your spirituality?

We said at the beginning of this section that you may wish to have your children score themselves. If you do, write each child's personal scores here.

Child _____

Characteristic   Importance

_____ intimacy average   _____ intimacy average

_____ passion average   _____ passion average

_____ commitment average   _____ commitment average

Child _____

Characteristic   Importance

_____ intimacy average   _____ intimacy average

_____ passion average   _____ passion average

_____ commitment average   _____ commitment average

Child _____

Characteristic   Importance

_____ intimacy average   _____ intimacy average

_____ passion average   _____ passion average

_____ commitment average   _____ commitment average

We strongly recommend that you note the following from your children's scores.

◆ Notice particularly any areas where a child scored him- or herself lower in Characteristic than in Importance. Think about what you can do to help your child grow spiritually in that area.

◆ Keep this workbook, and at least once a year have your children rate themselves again. Note the areas where they grow and where they weaken. Make it your job to help them in any area of weakness.

PART TWO: GROWING IN SPIRITUALITY TOGETHER AS A MARRIED COUPLE

Many couples strive for emotional intimacy (as they should) but never realize the rapture available to them if they were to add to their emotional intimacy the transforming power of spiritual intimacy. Joe Beam guides married couples to achieving that ecstasy in *Becoming ONE: Emotionally, Spiritually, Sexually*. We strongly recommend that book for every married couple along with its accompanying workbook, *Becoming ONE: Exercises in Intimacy*.

If you can get the *Becoming ONE* book and workbook, skip the following exercise and work through those when you finish this workbook. If possible, enroll in the *Becoming ONE* seminar.

If you prefer not to pursue that path, please answer the following questions.

1. How could you use Bible study to increase your spiritual unity as a couple?

2. How could you use prayer to increase your spiritual unity as a couple?

3. How could you involve yourselves and your family in church activities to increase your spiritual unity as a couple?

4. What will you commit to do to grow together in God?

5. When will you start?

We designed the exercises in this chapter to bring family members closer together. Be aware that as you incorporate younger family members into these exercises, they may react with resentment if the sessions are too long. Therefore, we recommend that you set a maximum time limit (appropriate for your family members' ages and temperaments) for each session. It's better to have two sessions or to slightly speed up a project to finish in a prescribed time limit than to turn these exercises into dreaded drudgery. Have fun! If everyone is enjoying themselves, let a session run longer. Remember, these exercises are made for your family, not your family for these exercises!

◆ ◆ ◆

EXERCISE 2:
SIX STEPS TO GO FROM THEORY TO PRACTICE

In *Fantastic Families* we list six steps to take you from theory to practice.

Step 1—Traditions and rituals

Step 2—Religious heritage

Step 3—Prayer and meditation

Step 4—Everyday life

Step 5—Study

Step 6—Avoiding dissension

In this exercise we concentrate on just one of those six ideas, though completing this exercise will definitely incorporate all the other five ideas. We recommend that your family outline a family night as a tradition and ritual. Make the outline this week although you may not be able to try implementing the outline until you complete other projects begun in previous chapters. If so, that's okay: We don't want you overwhelmed! When you've agreed on the outline with all its particulars and pick a beginning date, try it for at least four weeks. If it doesn't work as you hoped, modify it as needed and try it four more weeks. If it helps the family in spiritual ways, make it a perpetual ritual that your family does every week from now on.

To help you, we give you an example from a real family in North Augusta, South Carolina. They used the family night for many, many years with great success. When you've finished reading what they did, we'll give you a few suggestions for outlining your own family night.

A SPECIAL TRADITION TO CREATE COMMUNICATION

In *Fantastic Families* we tell of a tradition of the Thompson family. We asked them to share with us how others could implement that very powerful tradition into their families. They gave us pages and pages of information that we've summarized for you below.

The family's goals for Thompson Family Night were to develop open family communication, create warm family memories, instill a sense of family identity, teach manners, social etiquette, and respect, and to train their children in righteousness.

Every week they consistently created their tradition. All their children—three sons—are grown now, and *every one* of them has instituted a similar family night in his home!

THE THOMPSON FAMILY NIGHT

1. Mealtime

- Every person committed to family night and was held to his or commitment. Barry and Karen decided that their consistency in honoring family night would teach a valuable lesson to their children. Even when other important matters came up, they felt their example to their children was more important than the temporary intrusion of another matter into their lives.

- Karen had the kids help her make sure the house was clean and uncluttered before Barry came home from work. She then cooked a "family favorite" meal while directing her sons on how to set the table correctly with the "good" china and cloth napkins. She designated certain weeks where one family member was specially honored by allowing him to choose the menu.

- Each week Karen was seated next to a different son who was taught how to treat her with respect and honor. After the meal started, she was not allowed to leave the table. Either the dad or one of the sons served the table.

- Barry gave special emphasis to teaching his sons how to properly use silverware, napkins, etc. He helped them learn the art of polite table conversation including the all important "please" and "thank you."

- Except for perishable food items, no table clean-up occurred at the end of the meal. Barry and Karen would do that later after their sons were in bed. Rather than cleaning the table, they moved into the family room for their Bible study.

2. Bible Study

- ◆ When the children were smaller, Barry read from a Bible storybook. As they became older, he moved to reading stories from the Old Testament. He looked for age-appropriate stories and read them to the whole family from an easy-to-understand translation such as the New International Version. Each family night he read one story slowly in a clear voice. When the children became old enough, he would assign one of them to read the story, helping the child with pronunciations and public reading skills. (He wanted them to learn how to address an audience with poise and confidence.)

- ◆ Every lesson included applications made by Barry or Karen. Most lessons contained an application from the New Testament. Barry made sure the New Testament verses or truths related well to the Old Testament story the family had just shared.

- ◆ After the reading, Barry encouraged his sons to participate in discussion about the story, the application, and their views of what they were discussing.

- ◆ Though Barry was the primary teacher, he modeled great respect and honor to his wife, teaching the boys to do the same.

3. Praying Time

- ◆ When the Bible study time ended, each person prayed. To help the sons learn to pray, they were sometimes directed to write a list of the things they wanted to talk about with God. Barry and Karen made sure that the prayers weren't too long. As Karen says, "Short prayers are best for those with short attention spans."

4. Sharing Time

- ◆ After prayers, each person shared what was going on in his or her life. They might play a band instrument, recite memory work from school or church, or tell about something from school. At the Thompson house this segment sometimes ended with the family singing together.

5. Planning Time

- ◆ At the end of their family night, they discussed plans for the coming week like work projects or scheduled fun times. Karen kept a family calendar so everyone could know what was to happen and when. They also made longer-term plans like vacations and trips.

- ◆ During this ending segment Karen would occasionally bring up her disappointments or discipline problems that had not been resolved and needed to be addressed by the entire family. This created more of a sense of responsibility among all the sons and kept small problems from escalating into major problems.

Barry and Karen told me of some special things that came from Thompson Family Night.

A few years after getting started with family night, some friends gave us a beautiful Wolford oil lamp, which we made the special Family Night Lamp. We decided this lamp was to stand for the light of the love of Jesus and our love for each other. It became very significant and a sign of our unity as a family. When our boys came back from college for holidays and vacations, the lamp would be lighted and standing on the living room mantle, welcoming them home. It was one more way of saying "you're special; we love you."

We taught our children from the book of Kings the dangers of marrying ungodly people well before they were old enough to become emotionally involved. Later in their lives, during the week before each son's wedding (as you know, we only had sons), we had a family night with the prospective bride present. Barry read passages related to the husband/wife relationship, and each family member gave the engaged couple a "charge"[4] and a blessing. Then they were presented with their own family lamp—a copy of the one we have. Each couple has used their lamp, starting their own family night and also lighting it for gatherings in their home.

Notice that the Thompsons' family night had distinct sessions:

1. Mealtime
2 Bible Study
3. Praying Time
4. Sharing Time
5. Planning Time

1. Discuss the type of sessions you'd like to have in your family night. When you've come to consensus, write them here:

2. Within each of the sessions, the Thompsons had specific goals they wanted to accomplish for the family and for their children's futures. Using the sessions you listed above as headings, write here what your family wishes to accomplish in each session.

3. Now, for the last steps.

   a. What specific things should be included in each session to accomplish those goals? Put them here (again using session titles as headings).

   b. Now, write all you've put above into one document and then assign each responsibility to someone in the family. Make sure that copies of the completed document—including all assignments—are distributed well before you conduct your first family night.

   c. Choose the date you will implement the outline for at least a four-week tryout. Put the date on your family calendar and have fun with family night!

FAMILY AT WORK ▸ *Putting It to Work—Six Suggestions for Your Family*

As custom, we close this chapter by referring you to the six ideas for your family at the end of the corresponding chapter in *Fantastic Families*.

1. Set aside fifteen to thirty minutes each day for meditation and prayer.
2. Join a discussion group, or form one with your friends.
3. Use the Bible and its wonderful life lessons to help your children clarify their values.
4. Identify weaknesses and strengths.
5. Have family devotionals on a regular basis.
6. Volunteer your time and muscle and money to a cause.

When you implement your tryout of the family night you outlined in the previous exercise, you will already be doing activities 2, 3, and 5. Congratulations! You've already figured out how to use 50 percent of our ideas!

That leaves only three to choose from to do this week.

1. SET ASIDE TIME FOR PERSONAL MEDITATION AND PRAYER

If the family agrees to this as the idea to implement this week, everyone who is mature enough to read, meditate, and pray on his or her own should be given a calendar. Each day each person marks on his or her personal calendar the time of day and the length of time spent in this personal devotion. During family meeting or family night, each person should present his or her calendar for inspection by all other family members. By doing that you accomplish two things.

1. Everyone remains motivated to remember and make time for devotional every day.
2. Everyone in the family can share together the assurance that every other person takes spiritual well-being seriously.

As you begin your family night devotional, give reading assignments every person can do during the week in his or her personal devotion time that will prepare the entire family for the topic that week.

2. IDENTIFY WEAKNESSES AND STRENGTHS

This idea works best when family members have a great relationship and a wonderful ability to communicate without fighting, pouting, or withdrawing. If you doubt that your family, or any person in it, will do well with this activity, please choose another.

If you vote to do this one, have each person start by sharing what he believes his or her spiritual strengths are. One by one go around the room and as each person shares, other family members may comment at the person's conclusions about any other strengths—particular spiritual strengths—they've noticed. Make that session as positive as it can be.

When the strengths have been introduced in this manner, allow the first person to begin again. This time he or she discusses weaknesses in his or her spiritual life. If a glaring weakness goes unmentioned, other family members may point it out if

- ◆ they do it gently

- ◆ they do it kindly

- ◆ they do it with pure motives

When all the weaknesses for a person have been mentioned, the family gives encouragement and suggestions on how to improve the weakness or make it a strength.

Finally, the discussion moves to spiritual strengths and weaknesses of the family as a whole. Begin with a general discussion of weaknesses, combined with suggestions on how the weaknesses may be overcome. End with a happy session of discussing family strengths and why each person believes those strengths exist. Feel free to give honor to whom honor is due during this closing session.

3. VOLUNTEER

If your family votes to choose this activity, have everyone suggest the areas where your family's volunteering may do the most good in a spiritual sense. When everyone has made his or her suggestion, have a general discussion until a consensus is reached. When you decide what to do, make sure that you

- ◆ assign a family member to be responsible for arranging everything for the family's participation

- ◆ set a date that you will do it

One way the parent(s) in the family can volunteer to help other families grow is by becoming a facilitator and leading them through this course. See page vii.

HELPING OTHERS

You will immediately see that instead of "spiritual well-being," the following chart is titled Family Wellness. Don't be confused: Drs. Stinnett and DeFrain found spiritual well-being to be one of the six characteristics of strong families. Apparently to keep from offending any of their constituents, the Family/School/Partnership altered this characteristic to family wellness. Just as in previous chapters you chose activities that made sense to you and ignored those that didn't, do so in this chapter. Because we've included their suggestions for age-level activities in each chapter, we opted to use them in this chapter as well, even with their alterations.

We recommend that you add appropriate spiritual suggestions of your own in each age category. For example, when they suggest "making choices/setting priorities" for grades 4–5, you could make that more spiritual by changing it to "making godly choices and setting spiritual priorities." Similarly, "practicing refusal skills" could be expanded to "learning the difference in right and wrong, and practice refusing the wrong." We gave you a couple of suggestions but felt you would benefit in at least two ways from making the transitions yourself.

1. Because you know each individual's capability, you can make the suggested activities both challenging and doable for that person.

2. You can specifically tailor the activities to your own spiritual priorities and understandings.

Of course, some of their suggestions fit very well with spiritual well-being, even some that might not appear to at first glance. For example, when the chart suggests for grades 6–8 that there could be "exploring society's rules/values," a strongly religious family might react negatively. If you feel that way, perhaps you should think about it from a different perspective. If you are teaching your children beliefs and values that you hold dear, wouldn't it be a good thing to have them contemplate the values of the world *while they are still at home and can talk them through with you?* Sometimes kids don't reason as well as they should, and it would be a positive experience to have a calm, logical talk with other siblings and parents who can help them think through consequences attached to values and behaviors. So even that suggestion has merit in helping others grow spiritually.

We pray that this chapter leads you to activities that bless your lives. In the next chapter—learning to cope with stress and crises—we'll find out how to apply many of the things you've already learned.

Family Wellness

- ◆ Sharing values, goals, priorities
- ◆ Fostering wellness, safety, nutrition
- ◆ Developing a sense of morality
- ◆ Growing in spirituality
- ◆ Growing in self-esteem

Prenatal/Birth	Infancy
Nutrition/exercise	Establishing routines
	Safe environment
	Eating solid foods
	Praising positive behavior
	Appropriate clothing

Preschool–Kindergarten	Kindergarten–Grade 3
Learning acceptable behavior/ modeling values	Individual time table for growth
Self-care/body control	Selecting nutritious foods
Body privacy/protection	Developing conscience/ self-control
Eating different foods	Gentle supportive guidance
Developing talents/abilities	Learning about drugs/alcohol
	Practice just saying no

Grades 4–5	Grades 6–8
Making choices/setting priorities	Exploring society's rules/values
Eating healthy foods	Participating in community activities
Expanding drug/alcohol education	Planning family meals
Practicing refusal skills	Staying drug free
Exercising for fitness	Responsible moral behavior

Respecting parental rules	Understanding gender role
Internalizing rules of behavior	
Praising achievements	

Grades 9–12	**Early Adult**
Planning long term goals	Starting a family
Maintaining physical/mental health	Developing parenting skills
Applying consumer skills in food selection	Developing appropriate support systems/communications
Identifying ethical principles	Establishing traditions for the new family
Value-based choices	Responsibility for elderly
Personal integrity	Fostering mental health
Learning parenting skills	

Middle Adult	**Later Adult**
Changing family functions	Selecting and adapting appropriate housing
Networking with the extended family	Adapting lifestyle to maintain good health
Accepting and adjusting to career changes	Monitoring prescribed medication
Dealing with loss/grief	Maintaining positive mental health
Preventative health care/ maintenance	Continuing good nutrition habits
	Volunteering or considering part-time employment
	Using community resources
	Family recreation
	Choosing medical specialists and helpers

	Understanding care-giving principles
	Adapting to children's traditions

STEP SIX
LEARN TO COPE
WITH STRESS AND CRISES

We all tell each other to do it, but could it be that nobody's listening? We hear the words constantly:

"Lighten up!" our friends say.

"In a hundred years, it won't matter. Why get so uptight about it now?" whisper our coworkers.

"Don't worry. Be happy!" chirps that cheerful little song on the radio.

"Relax; everything's going to be okay," coos the dentist.

"We're from the government; we're here to help you," smiles the man taking a calculator from his briefcase.

Well, maybe we went a little overboard with that last one, but you get the idea. Joe Beam once received a fax with only these words on it:

> Dear Joe,
>
> I can run things just fine by myself—without your help. You'd be a lot happier if you quit acting as if the weight of the world were on *your* shoulders, and I wouldn't have to worry so much about you!
>
> Love, God

No one ever owned up to sending it, but Joe's pretty sure that God nodded in agreement as he watched whoever it was type it.

Why do we get so uptight? Why has the gastrointestinal distress caused by human stress created a worldwide multibillion dollar pharmaceutical windfall? What is it about us that is slowly but surely killing us?

When God designed the human body, he equipped it with marvelous biological weapons and deep-seated instincts designed to help us survive. Whether he made Adam and Eve that way at the beginning or altered them in some way as they left the garden, he didn't leave them defenseless to the seen and unseen worlds that would evermore be dangerous for them. Some of the animals they could have petted the day before were now threats to their very existence. Disease and aging, previously unknown, became reality. From the moment Adam and Eve were driven from their idyllic habitat, they were beset by dangers from within and without themselves.

INSTINCT OF ACTION

Within the package of instincts God created for us, he neatly placed what is often called the "fight or flight" reaction. Most of us have heard of it, and probably all of us have experienced it. When confronted by what we sense as a danger or threat, we flush with adrenaline and either attack it (if we think we have a chance of winning) or run for our lives (if we think we have no chance of winning). Thus, "fight" or "flight."

Interestingly, not as many people are familiar with the failure that sometimes occurs during that instinctive reaction.

Freeze.

It's that middle ground between fight (attack!) and flight (run!). Overwhelmed to the point of not knowing what to do, the person simply freezes and does nothing. No fighting. No fleeing. Just freezing. The adrenaline flows; the nervous system kicks into high gear; but no external action takes place.

As you might imagine, freezing can lead to many kinds of physiological and psychological problems.

It's easy to see the problem in a situation like freezing when looking up to see a bus barreling down on you. We all know the probable results of that instinct failure. But in this chapter we consider a type of instinctive failure that isn't so easily recognized as the "deer in the headlight" type failure. It's freezing in the face of dangers we perceive (either consciously or subconsciously) because we feel *compelled* not to do anything. We know *what* to do and *could* do it, but choose to do nothing.

INSTINCT OF INACTION

In our modern society the majority of us don't have many situations where we are physically threatened. It happens, but it isn't the norm. Not many kids fear that their teacher is going to chase them around the classroom with a bullwhip. (Okay, maybe you do, but not many kids do.) And not many employees fear that their supervisor is going to drag them outside and thrash them with a large stick if a deadline is missed. Even most marriages aren't violent, which means that one mate isn't fearing physical retaliation from the other.

The threats more typically reacted to in our culture are those that cannot be physically responded to. Money problems. Worry about our kids' new friends. Illness. Change of ownership where we work. We get uptight and ready for action, but there isn't a whole lot we can do to burn off the chemicals created by our bodies as we prepare to face the threat. We have no definite and immediate path to confront the threat.

The situation where we more likely can react as we've been designed is when we consciously or subconsciously perceive a threat from another human. That seems to happen most often during interpersonal conflict. When we get into conflict with another person—teacher, parent, spouse, boss, friend, sibling—our bodies prepare themselves for fighting or fleeing. Understand that fighting doesn't necessarily mean fisticuffs; it means an activity that immediately and directly confronts the threat so that two things can happen. First, the threat is diminished or removed. Second, the mind and body can focus on some kind of action so that adrenaline can be used up. So when conflict arises we can either immediately and directly go into action to resolve it or run away by actually fleeing the situation.

We usually do neither.

Why?

Sometimes it's because we feel powerless. "Well, he's the teacher and there's nothing I can do," or "The boss isn't always right but she's always the boss."

Sometimes it's because we don't want to risk alienation. "If I do something about this, she may not be my friend anymore."

Other times it's a fear of escalating the conflict. "I know I should do something, but if I do, it *really* will be a fight."

It can even be our own sense of responsibility. "I know I let myself be talked into taking on too much, but there's nothing I can do about it now. I'll just have to tough it out."

We don't fight. We don't run. We just freeze. And the adrenaline keeps building in our system. It's joined by other chemicals our bodies create to prepare us to deal with the perceived threat. We're prepared to fight or run, but we do neither and that causes stress. That stress negatively affects us in emotional and physical ways that lead to problems as wide ranging as elevated blood pressure, acid reflux, numbness, panic attacks, rapid pulse, depression, and on and on and on.

INSTINCT EFFECTS ON FAMILIES

So, what has all this to do with strong families?

We're glad you asked that question.

Families aren't immune to stress. Every crisis in life immediately creates the fight, flight, or freeze reaction—including crises that involve the family. Chronic situations (not a crisis but a lasting dilemma) lead to stress in the family. If you want your family to be strong, you must develop ways to deal with crises (short-term situations) and stress (longer lasting situations).

Unfortunately, stress reaches across all life situations. Stress at work or school often creates stress in the family. On the other hand, stress in the family very definitely can create stress at work or school. Adrenaline and all the other chemicals manufactured by the body to combat perceived threats don't stay at the office or the home; they flow through the body wherever that body goes.

Just as stress debilitates the human body, it debilitates the body of joined people we call family. Every person in the family, and the family as a unit, must learn to cope.

◆ ◆ ◆

EXERCISE 1:
SIX TACTICS FOR COPING WITH STRESS

As in every previous chapter, the first exercise is primarily for the parent(s). And, as custom, you may involve older, mature children in this exercise if you wish.

We believe that children tend to emulate the modeled behavior of their parent(s). If you want your children to learn to cope with the crises that crash into life from time to time or to live without crippling stress, you must first learn to control stress yourself.

In *Fantastic Families* we suggest six tactics for coping with stress.

Tactic #1—Keep things in perspective

Tactic #2—Let go and let God

Tactic #3—Focus on something bigger than self

Tactic #4—Humor yourself

Tactic #5—Take one step at a time

Tactic #6—Refresh and restore

In this workbook we ask you to focus on tactics 5 and 6.

TAKE ONE STEP AT A TIME

In *Fantastic Families* we suggested that taking one step at a time means minimizing fragmentation and prioritizing. Several years ago Joe Beam sat in a seminar taught by experts whose specialty was helping salespeople overcome call reluctance. One of the presenters drew a large M on a flip chart and said, "Let that M stand for your motivation." He then drew an arrow and at its point wrote a large G. "That G stands for your goal. The way I just drew it is the way it's supposed to be. Strong motivation (the M), with a clear goal (the G), and a definite path (the arrow) to reach that goal. Problem is, most of you guys aren't doing this."

Of course, we all sat quietly waiting for the punch line. Never interrupt a speaker when he's about to make his point, or you'll be the one called on to answer the questions nobody can answer.

"You guys are probably more like this." He then took another sheet, drew a large M, but instead of one arrow, he drew about a dozen smaller arrows reaching out from the M. When he finished it looked as if the M had pointed porcupine quills completely surrounding it, pointing to all 360 degrees of the compass. Then methodically at the end of each arrow he drew a little g.

"You see, you have motivation. But what you don't have is a clear goal. Understand? You're drawn in so many directions you'll never succeed at any of them."

He slowly scanned the room looking for any objection. He didn't know all of us, but he was pretty sure of himself because of one very simple but very common fact. Most of us live our lives full of small goals that have little to do with each other. We're seldom succeeding at one because we're constantly drawn to another.

Hmmm. Think that could be true of you as a parent—the head of your family?

For this exercise we ask each of you to answer the following questions.

1. What are the goals in your life that really are important to you? (List every important goal here. If it really isn't important to you, don't write it.)

2. Arrange these goals in order of priority to you. The one you want most becomes number 1. Write them in order until you have them all.

3. How would changing the priorities you listed above reduce stress in your life? (Take your time here. Pray for wisdom. Where are the areas that create stress for you, and how important are those areas to you really? What are the "threats" in each situation, and what do your true priorities reveal to you about how to deal with those threats? In other words, what should you quit worrying about and relegate to a less important position in your life?)

4. If you received any insight from your answers to the question above, what will you do to decrease the stress in your life?

REFRESH AND RESTORE

Notice that tactic 6, refresh and restore, in the book *Fantastic Families* suggests three options: getting outside, exercising, and enjoying pets. One thing all three options have in common is the ability to help calm your body from the fight or flight state. They give you something to do immediately and directly that removes your focus from the "threat." Exercise adds the wonderful dimension of actually using up adrenaline and other chemicals your body produced. If you went around having fisticuffs with anyone who caused you to have a fight or flight syndrome, you would naturally burn away the adrenaline produced by the syndrome. The same thing would happen if you fled for your life at breakneck speed from a bruiser who decided to do a little pummeling on you. But godly (and civilized) people don't act like that. The next best thing is to find another method for removing the extra energy.

Why not figure a way to do all three options at the same time? Get a pet that loves the outdoors and go exercise. We see people briskly walking their dogs all hours of the day and night and think that's a marvelous stress-reducing activity. (We occasionally see small people being dragged by their Great Danes, but we think it likely doesn't provide as much exercise when you're clinging to a leash and begging for your dog to stop so that you can stand up. Therefore, we do not recommend that particular method of dog walking.) With a little imagination and a bit of dedication, you can find a way to manage the stress in your life by refreshing and restoring.

1. What will you do regularly to refresh and restore yourself to manage your stress?

2. What will you do—beyond your regular routine—when you find yourself stressed about a situation?

We designed the exercises in this chapter to bring family members closer together. Be aware that as you incorporate younger family members into these exercises, they may react with resentment if the sessions are too long. Therefore, we recommend that you set a maximum time limit (appropriate for your family members' ages and temperaments) for each session. It's better to have two sessions or to slightly speed up a project to finish in a prescribed time limit than to turn these exercises into dreaded drudgery. Have fun! If everyone is enjoying themselves, let a session run longer. Remember, these exercises are made for your family, not your family for these exercises!

◆ ◆ ◆

EXERCISE 2:
STRATEGIES FOR SURVIVING

You recall that we've been saying that stress typically results from longer-lasting situations while a crisis is usually shorter lived. That's why the skills for coping with stress can help one get through a crisis, but more is needed. In times of intense emotion, other skills help considerably.

We recommend six strategies for surviving stress in *Fantastic Families*.

Strategy #1—See the roses among the thorns

Strategy #2—Pull together

Strategy #3—Go get help

Strategy #4—Use spiritual resources

Strategy #5—Open channels of communication

Strategy #6—Go with the flow

We obviously don't want to create a crisis so you can practice each of these six strategies. Therefore, the exercise we lead you through will help you look backward to a past crisis so that you can be better prepared for future crises. You can do this by applying strategy #1 above—seeing roses among the thorns.

Several years ago Ron Willingham offered a course to churches called *Adventures in Christian Living*. In one of the sessions people shared a past event in their lives that they thought at the time was a terrible tragedy but that they now look back at and see its hidden blessings. In every church that conducted the course, it was the most powerful topic. Without exception, every adult told of some awful thing that eventually held a blessing beyond measure.

One lady told of a time in her childhood when she tried to intervene in a vicious fight between her mother and father. As they struggled with each other, she stepped between them just as they knocked a hot frying pan of grease off the stove. Her head was scalded to the point that she would never grow hair again. As she told her story, she said, "People always compliment my hair. It's not mine in the sense that I grew it. I praise God that we have the money to buy very, very well done wigs. What's the blessing in this? The first may seem trivial to you, but I never have to worry about doing my hair. I just put it on! The second is much more meaningful. My husband and my daughters have seen me on many occasions without the wig...just the scars and tufts. In a world where you wonder if people would love you if they could see the 'warts and all,' I know. My husband and my daughters love me just the way I am. Scars and all. I'd say that's quite a blessing, wouldn't you?"

Others told of unexpected blessings that came with handicapped children, financial reversal, or the death of someone they loved. The situations were all different, but results were the same: "We know that in all things God works for the good of those who love him, who have been called according to his purpose" (Romans 8:28).

In this exercise we ask the parent(s) to speak first. Be very open, honest, and transparent with your family. Tell of some very painful or overwhelming crisis in your life that brought a wonderful blessing. We're not encouraging you to be melodramatic, but we are asking you to let your children see your true emotions. Relive the event as you describe it. Allow yourself to luxuriate in the blessing that came from it.

Then open the floor to your children. Encourage each to think of something —no matter how large or small—that was a crisis for them but led to a blessing. Maybe they gained an awareness or knowledge that will help them as they grow older. Maybe they met a new friend. Maybe they became Christians. The parent(s) should help any child who cannot think of an earlier crisis. Ask gentle questions to help each child think it through.

As each person finishes, ask the family to respond with positive comments by asking general questions. "What does that story teach you?" or "How does what we just heard help us prepare for the future?"

If your family has gone through a crisis together, have each person tell how he or she felt as it occurred. Then have each person tell the blessing he or she got from it.

As you prepare for this family session, work through the following questions.

1. What is a crisis that I endured that turned out to be a blessing?

2. How did I feel when the crisis was occurring?

3. How do I feel about the blessing that came from it?

4. What crisis did we endure as a family that turned out to contain a blessing?

5. How did I feel about it as it occurred?

6. How do I feel about the blessing that came from it?

FAMILY AT WORK ▶ *Putting It to Work—Six Suggestions for Your Family*

As we end this chapter, we again refer you to the "Putting It to Work" section of *Fantastic Families*. There we offered these six ideas:

1. Assess the stress in your life.
2. Commit yourself to an exercise program.

3. Cultivate your sense of humor.
4. Select a hobby that refreshes and pleases you.
5. Periodically review plans concerning death.
6. Use television and movies as a catalyst for family discussions.

Rather than allowing the family to choose an activity for this week, we ask you to combine numbers 3 and 6 in the following way.

Have a humor period at least once a week. It doesn't have to be long—it can be done during dinner—or it may occasionally be an entire evening of entertainment. Just make sure that one person is assigned to "bring the humor" for every week.

Here are some examples of short versions that can be done as you linger over dessert.

- Have someone read two or three poems by Shel Silverstein. (The Beam family particularly finds great humor in his book *Where the Sidewalk Ends*.)

- Ask someone to read a chapter from any of Dave Barry's books. (Slight editing may be needed by a parent.) Joe Beam laughed so hard reading one of Dave Barry's books on an airplane that the flight attendant threatened to take it away from him for the benefit of the other passengers! (Joe never doubted she just wanted a book that funny for herself.)

- Play a portion of a comedy audio or video cassette. (Just make sure it is suitable for your family.)

A visit to your local bookstore or library should give you plenty of material for your humor session.

If you prefer, every so often you can have talent night. Give each family member a week or so to do something like write a joke, create a comedy skit, develop a stand-up routine, write a funny song, etc. Make sure that everyone knows that no one is expecting professional talent and that no one should take the night too seriously. It should be a night of fun and frolic.

Some families would benefit from having older relatives over to tell of funny things that happened throughout their lives—especially anything that involved other relatives. If you invite older relatives for a night of storytelling, be sure to record the oral history for your children's futures.

Another way to have a humor night is to rent funny movies that everyone can relate to. We like *Arsenic and Old Lace*, but we also admit a penchant for anything done by the Marx Brothers. Some of us even watched *The Gay 90s* over and over to learn the "Who's on First?" routine by Abbot and Costello to present at a family gathering. It failed when the other person forgot the routine and answered the lead-in "Who's on first?" with "I think it was Mark McGuire."

So much for that routine.

As you can see, the whole idea is to have fun. Why? Because laughter reduces stress. It burns adrenaline. It makes the heart happy. It turns sorrow into joy.

Even with all the medicines available today, there is nothing that can match laughter.

After your family discusses how they would like to approach a humor session once a week, work through the following questions to develop your plans.

1. Who will be responsible for providing humor for each of the next four weeks? (List the dates and the specific person.)

2. How often will you have a humor night?

3. Who is responsible for planning humor nights?

4. On what dates will you have your first three humor nights?

5. What will you have for the first humor night? The second? The third?

6. What books, audio tapes, or videos have been suggested for use?

HELPING OTHERS

While not as dramatic as in step 5, the Family/School/Community Partnership made a small change in the way they list this strong family characteristic. They rephrased it "managing resources, crises, and stress." Since the management of resources can be a wonderful way to cope with stress and crises, we happily accept their minor change in wording and list all their ideas on the following chart without comment. As usual, use what you think valuable and ignore the rest.

Well, you've made it nearly to the end. The next chapter wraps up the weeks you've spent together intensely working on becoming a stronger family.

Managing Resources, Crises, and Stress

◆ Sharing and managing resources, including economics
◆ Resolving problems through decision making
◆ Supporting family/school/community networks
◆ Fostering conflict resolution

Prenatal/Birth	Infancy
Financial planning	Pooling resources
Planning for quality child care	Handling problems
	Flexible scheduling

Preschool–Kindergarten	Kindergarten–Grade 3
Managing transitions	Identify roles and responsibilities of family members
Encourage creative thinking	Caring for possessions
Using language to solve problems	Distinguishing between wants and needs
Sources of help for children/ family	Developing problem solving skills
Reinforcing positive behavior	Developing dialogue between family/school
	Consequences of actions

Grades 4–5	Grades 6–8
Involving children in family decision making	Managing personal resources
Managing time	Exploring personal values
Distinguishing human/non-human resources	Networking with school/ community
Networking with teachers/school	Demonstrating coping strategies
Sources of problems/conflicts	Resolving peer pressure

Stress reducers/relaxation techniques	Accepting constructive criticism
	Assisting in family decision making

Grades 9–12	Early Adult
Using barter	Reaffirming one's self-esteem
Budgeting financial resources	Setting realistic expectations and new roles
Value based consumer decisions/ opportunity cost/credit	Developing a sense of humor
Locating information resources	Family economics, investments
Adapting to change	

Middle Adult	Later Adult
Evaluating personal finances	Dealing with possessions
Building partnership and contractual agreements	Planning for financial security
Networking with community agencies and institutions	Using resources to assure financial security
Coping with work stresses	Paying for health care
Dealing with and resolving marital changes	Investing in health care/finding health care
	Assisting adult children
	Accepting care from adult children and others (role-reversal)
	Accepting limitations

BECOMING A
FANTASTIC FAMILY

You've had a lot of work to do over the last several weeks, and we want to be the first to congratulate you for sticking with it. We feel confident that you have grown individually and as a family. While no one course or workbook can be the panacea for every need, we know from the research of Drs. Stinnett and DeFrain that the six strengths you've been working on so diligently are crucial to family success.

How have you progressed with the goals your family set at the beginning? Wonderful! How have any goals been modified? That's good too. Growing families are dynamic families. That means that things constantly are in a state of movement. As things change, goals may need modification. Sometimes they even need to be abandoned and replaced by other goals altogether.

As you conclude this workbook, we ask you to complete two exercises very similar to the ones you completed in the introduction. As you do, you will help your family continue to grow into the future.

> **W**e designed the exercises in this chapter to bring family members closer together. Be aware that as you incorporate younger family members into these exercises, they may react with resentment if the sessions are too long. Therefore, we recommend that you set a maximum time limit (appropriate for your family members' ages and temperaments) for each session. It's better to have two sessions or to slightly speed up a project to finish in a prescribed time limit than to turn these exercises into dreaded drudgery. Have fun! If everyone is enjoying themselves, let a session run longer. Remember, these exercises are made for your family, not your family for these exercises!

EXERCISE 1:
DISCOVERING WHERE YOU ARE NOW

In the introduction we gave you the Family Strengths Assessment so that your family could get a "picture" of where you were as you started this course. Because you completed that assessment then, you have a perfect opportunity to see how your family has changed in the last eight weeks. The family members who complete the assessment now should be the same ones who completed it in the introduction. We remind you again that for those who either cannot read the statements or cannot yet comprehend every statement, another family member should read and explain the statements. *When explaining a statement, be careful not to inadvertently change its meaning!*

ASSESSING YOUR FAMILY'S STRENGTHS

Each family member should give his or her own answers for the questions below. (There is one exception: You will notice question 3 applies to husband and wife only.) Put an "S" for *strength* beside those qualities you feel your family has achieved, and a "G" for *growth* beside those qualities that are areas of potential growth. If the particular characteristic does not apply to your family or is not a characteristic important to you, put an "NA" for *not applicable.*

By doing this exercise, family members will be able to identify those areas they would like to work on together to improve and those areas of strength that will serve as the foundation for their growth and positive change together.

You will see that we have two blanks next to each statement. *Leave the first blank empty for now.* Put the S or G or NA in the blank closest to the statement (the blank on the right). The first blank on the left will be used later.

Please fill the following blanks with the correct information before completing the assessment.

Age_____

Sex_____

Number of parents living in the home_____

Number of children living in the home_____

Number of other relatives living in the home_____

When you have finished the entire assessment (including later instructions about what to do with the first blank on the left), we ask you to please send the above information and the answer sheet that follows to Family Dynamics Institute. You can either tear the sheets from this workbook or send us a copy. By doing so, you will help us in our research to know how to help the thousands of families we work with each year. Mail the copies for each family member in one envelope to FDI, P.O. Box 211668, Augusta, GA 30917. If you wish to include a list of the names of family members, we'll send you graduation certificates for each person that you may frame and proudly display.

COMMITMENT

1. _____ _____We are "always there" for each other.

2. _____ _____We are dedicated to our marriage as the core of the family.

3. _____ _____We (spouses) are faithful to each other sexually.

4. _____ _____We value each family member as a precious part of the family.

5. _____ _____We take care of each other and help each other.

6. _____ _____We share many family goals.

7. _____ _____We give family priority over outside activities, including work.

8. _____ _____We are honest with each other.

9. _____ _____We have numerous family traditions.

10. _____ _____We will endure/stay together as a family.

11. _____ _____We have unconditional love for each other.

12. _____ _____We can depend on each other.

13. _____ _____We make sacrifices for our family.

14. _____ _____Give an overall rating (S or G) of *commitment* in your family.

APPRECIATION AND AFFECTION

15. _____ _____We show appreciation to each other every day.

16. _____ _____We feel deep and genuine affection for each other.

17. _____ _____We avoid criticizing each other.

18. _____ _____We speak positively to each other.

19. _____ _____We recognize each other's accomplishments.

20. _____ _____We see each other's good qualities.

21. _____ _____We look for the good in each other (dig for diamonds).

22. _____ _____We are sincere in expressions of appreciation.

23. _____ _____We practice good manners at home and with others.

24. _____ _____We refrain from sarcasm and put-downs.

25. _____ _____We cultivate humor that is gentle and positive. (No one is embarrassed or hurt by it.)

26. _____ _____We accept compliments and kindnesses graciously.

27. _____ _____We create a pleasant environment at home.

28. _____ _____We enhance each other's self-esteem.

29. _____ _____We feel safe and secure in our interactions with each other.

30. _____ _____Give an overall rating (S or G) of *appreciation and affection* in your family.

POSITIVE COMMUNICATION

31. _____ _____We allow time for communication (conversations, discussions).

32. _____ _____We have positive communication.

33. _____ _____We listen to each other.

34. _____ _____We check the meaning of messages (give feedback, seek clarification).

35. _____ _____We see things from each other's point of view (have empathy).

36. _____ _____We avoid criticizing, judging, or acting superior.

37. _____ _____We are honest and truthful (and kind).

38. _____ _____We deal with disagreements promptly.

39. _____ _____We deal with conflict issues one at a time.

40. _____ _____We are specific when dealing with conflict issues.

41. _____ _____We seek compromise or consensus in resolving conflict (rather than "win or lose").

42. _____ _____We avoid actions and words that would be emotionally devastating to each other.

43. _____ _____We seek to understand and accept our differences.

44. _____ _____Give an overall rating (S or G) of *positive communication* in your family.

TIME TOGETHER

45. _____ _____We eat meals together regularly.

46. _____ _____We do house and yard chores together.

47. _____ _____We spend time together in recreation (play).

48. _____ _____We participate in religious activities together.

49. _____ _____We attend school or social activities together.

50. _____ _____We celebrate holidays, birthdays, and anniversaries as a family.

51. _____ _____We have a family vacation.

52. _____ _____We enjoy each other's company.

53. _____ _____We have good times together that are unplanned and spontaneous.

54. _____ _____We take time to be with each other.

55. _____ _____We spend good quality time together.

56. _____ _____Give an overall rating (S or G) of *time together* in your family.

SPIRITUAL WELL-BEING

57. _____ _____We believe that God has a purpose for our lives.

58. _____ _____We have moral beliefs and values that guide us (honesty, responsibility).

59. _____ _____We practice virtues such as patience, forgiveness, and controlling anger.

60. _____ _____We have inner peace even in difficult times because of our relationship with God.

61. _____ _____We have an outlook on life that is usually hopeful and confident.

62. _____ _____We believe that God watches over and guides our family.

63. _____ _____We are part of a church family.

64. _____ _____We have family and friends who share our spiritual beliefs.

65. _____ _____We praise God for his love and involvement in our family.

66. _____ _____We attend worship services as a family.

67. _____ _____We read and study the Bible and other Christian literature.

68. _____ _____We spend time each day in prayer.

69. _____ _____We meditate on God's Word.

70. _____ _____We apply our spiritual values to everyday life.

71. _____ _____We avoid extreme or ongoing arguments over beliefs.

72. _____ _____Give an overall rating (S or G) of *spiritual well-being* in your family.

ABILITY TO COPE WITH STRESS AND CRISES

73. _____ _____We are able to ignore petty irritants and minor stresses.

74. _____ _____We don't give lots of attention or energy to worry.

75. _____ _____We believe that daily struggles/challenges are just a part of reaching a bigger goal.

76. _____ _____We use humor to relieve stress and tension.

77. _____ _____We take life one day at a time.

78. _____ _____We eliminate some involvements when our schedules get too full.

79. _____ _____We give attention/energy to the most important things first.

80. _____ _____We engage in recreational activities and hobbies.

81. _____ _____We enjoy outdoor relaxation and recreation.

82. _____ _____We participate in regular exercise.

83. _____ _____We manage to see some good in bad situations.

84. _____ _____We work together to face the challenges of crises.

85. _____ _____We support each other emotionally in crisis situations.

86. _____ _____We seek help from friends, church, and neighbors during crises.

87. _____ _____We seek professional help in crisis situations.

88. _____ _____We call on spiritual resources (God's help, faith, hope) in times of crises.

89. _____ _____We see opportunities for personal and family growth in crisis situations.

90. _____ _____We use good communication to share feelings and to solve problems.

91. _____ _____We are flexible and adaptable.

92. _____ _____Give an overall rating (S or G) of *ability to cope with stress and crises* in your family.

To see how you have changed as a family (or at least how your perceptions have changed), we ask you to do a task that may seem a tad tedious but that can be *very* revealing. Use the first blank before each statement—the blank you left empty—to record the response you gave to each statement when you completed the survey as you worked through the introduction. Yes, we realize that it's awkward to switch between pages to jot your previous scores. But we encourage you to endure the few minutes of aggravation so that you can benefit from what you're about to learn.

When everyone has completed the survey and completed jotting their scores from the introduction, it's time for the family discussion.

As before, follow these ground rules for discussion:

- No one may be censured, criticized, or in any way made to feel bad because of the answers he or she gives.

- Everyone has permission to share what he or she really feels.

- Each person's feelings will be respected, even if he or she is the only person in the family to feel that way.

For these final discussions, we think it best that a parent be chairperson. Make sure that it is a parent considered by the majority to be fair and evenhanded.

1. Have each person tell how he or she scored the statement in the introductory session and then how he or she scores it now. If the scoring is different, ask the person to explain why. Take your time and let each person explain as much as he or she likes. Other family members may ask questions for clarification, but if anyone in any way indicates displeasure or disagreement, the chairperson *must* intervene. Openness and honesty must be honored. It is much more important to have family members share their real feelings than to try to force everyone to see things the same way.

2. Have someone in the family keep a tally sheet of the old scores and a tally sheet of the new scores.

3. When the discussion is finished, the chairperson makes a quick comparison of the tally sheet for the old questions to see that it is the same as the tally sheet from the introductory session. (This is simply a check and balance system to avoid mistakes.) Any imbalances should be adjusted to the original tally sheet.

4. The entire family examines the tally sheets to evaluate in which areas the family has grown the most and on which areas the family still needs to concentrate for more growth.

Write here the characteristic that your family improved the most.

Write here the characteristic that your family most needs to improve.

5.   The chairperson then asks which characteristic was listed in the introductory session as their family's weakest. Have the family discuss this question, "How have we changed in that characteristic? Be as specific as you can in examples and illustrations from our family life."

◆ ◆ ◆

EXERCISE 2:
SETTING GOALS

Now that you've examined how your family has changed in terms of the six healthy characteristics, it's time to specifically see your progress with the goals you set during the introductory session.

1.   Have the goal read from that session and then have each family member discuss how he or she feels the family has done in accomplishing that goal.

2.   When that discussion is finished, ask the general question, "How could we have accomplished that goal more effectively?"

3.   Now it's time to make goals for the future. The chairperson asks every person to take from five to ten minutes to list three specific goals they would like for the family to accomplish that would overcome the weakest characteristic. As before, the goals may be generic ("let's be happier") or more specific ("let's buy a new Suburban").

4.   When everyone is finished, the chairperson has each individual share one goal. The secretary records the goals. As each goal is shared, others may ask clarification questions, but no one may indicate any negative attitude about the goal in any way. The chairperson must intervene if anyone does.

5.   After the first round, two more rounds take place in the same manner.

6.   When finished, the secretary reads all the goals slowly so that everyone is reminded of what each goal is.

7.   After the reading, the chairperson calls for a vote to determine the three goals that the family will work on.

8. Once the three goals are established, the family discusses each one in detail. Each goal must be honed to answer the following questions.

- ◆ How can we make this goal specific enough so that we will know when we actually accomplish it? (For example, how would you know you had become "happier"? What criteria would let you know that you had become happier?)

- ◆ What date will the family agree on for completing this goal?

- ◆ How could the family measure the incremental accomplishment of this goal? (For example, if you intend to have a goal accomplished within six months, how can you measure how much of the goal you've achieved during each of the intervening months?)

9. When the family agrees on the three goals and those goals have been honed to meet the above criteria, write the three goals in the space provided.

a. Specific family goal number 1:

We will accomplish this goal by this date: _____.
The way we will measure our progress in the meantime is

b. Specific family goal number 2:

We will accomplish this goal by this date: _____.
The way we will measure our progress in the meantime is

c. Specific family goal number 3:

d. We will accomplish this goal by this date: _____

The way we will measure our progress in the meantime is

Putting It to Work—Six Ideas for Your Family

Now, as you close, it's time to thank each other. The last exercise we give you is to write a specific letter of appreciation or admiration to every other person in your family. Everything you write must be positive and uplifting.

Please use the following guides to begin each paragraph in your letter to each person.

> I am so happy you are in this family because...
> Something I always want you to remember is...
> I appreciate how you've helped our family grow recently by...
> My pledge to you is...

Set a meeting time when the letters will be exchanged. After convening the meeting, have each person hand deliver his or her letters to everyone else in the family. The chair tells the family when to open their letters and start reading. Of course, someone may need to read to younger family members (just as they will have already helped them write their letters.)

After every letter is read, have someone again read The Family Declaration of Commitment you made during chapter 1. Have every person verbally pledge his or her intent to honor that commitment and then end your meeting with a prayer session. Allow every person to pray who wishes to pray. Hold hands if comfortable.

The parent who ends the prayer should entreat not only God's protection and guidance but also that the family will always be bound together by love and will always continue to grow together.

Amen.

◆ NOTES ◆

INTRODUCTION

1. *Webster's New Universal Unabridged Dictionary* (New York: Barnes & Noble Books, 1996), 781.

CHAPTER 1. STEP ONE ◆ COMMIT TO YOUR FAMILY

1. Matthew 7:24–27.

2. Joe Beam, *Becoming ONE, Emotionally, Spiritually, Sexually* (West Monroe, La.: Howard Publishing, 1999). This book and accompanying workbook, *Exercises in Intimacy*, are part of the materials for the powerful and dynamic couples' interactive eight-week seminar, *Becoming ONE*. For more information, call 1-800-650-9995.

3. Please note that we designed this workbook for more than one type of family. We offer it to strengthen traditional, single-parent, or blended families. This exercise applies specifically to homes where a married couple lives with children—whether they are both natural parents or one is a stepparent. We are not ignoring single parents with this exercise. It is certainly applicable if they decide to marry.

4. The Family/School/Community Partnership, Florida Department of Education, Division of Vocational, Adult, Community Education, Home Economics Section. An Executive Summary of the program by Virginia Bert and Kathleen Funderburk. This chart is applied to each of the strong family characteristics and is used in the corresponding chapters throughout this workbook.

CHAPTER 2. STEP TWO ◆ EXPRESS APPRECIATION AND AFFECTION

1. Luke 17:17–19.

2. *Webster's New Universal Unabridged Dictionary*, 103.

3. Ibid., 33.

4. Willard Harley, Jr., *Five Steps to Romantic Love: A Guide for Readers of Love Busters and His Needs, Her Needs* (Grand Rapids, Mich.: Fleming H. Revell, 1993), 88.

CHAPTER 3. STEP THREE ◆ SHARE POSITIVE COMMUNICATION

1. *Webster's New Universal Unabridged Dictionary*, 414.

2. Ibid.

3. Developed and copyrighted by Joe Beam. © 2000. This model may not be used without written consent from Joe Beam. He may be contacted at Family Dynamics Institute; P.O. Box 211668; Augusta, GA 30917-1668.

4. Stated during Dr. Braund's live radio interview of Joe Beam, February 22, 2000.

5. Contact Family Dynamics Institute at 1-800-650-9995 for information about this two-and-a-half-hour seminar that can be purchased for $75 and used repeatedly. It contains videos, audios, reproducible handouts, and invitation postcards. This seminar is aimed specifically at married couples, but the principle applies to any individuals in conflict.

6. Joe Beam allows his model to be used in your family as long as you only reproduce it for family members for this specific activity.

CHAPTER 4. STEP FOUR ◆ SPEND TIME TOGETHER

1. *Webster's New Universal Unabridged Dictionary*, 1579.

CHAPTER 5. STEP FIVE ◆ NURTURE SPIRITUAL WELL-BEING

1. John Gottman and Nan Silver, *The Seven Principles for Making Marriage Work* (New York: Crown Publishers, 1999), 243–245.

2. For more discussion on this, see Robert J. Sternberg, *Cupid's Arrow* (Cambridge: Cambridge University Press, 1998).

3. We liberally borrowed from a survey presented in *Becoming ONE: Exercises in Intimacy* (West Monroe, La.: Howard Publishing, 1999), 10, which we used with special permission from Dr. Robert Sternberg at Yale University. We took only a few of those statements and modified them from his purpose of measuring love in a couple's relationship to our purpose of taking a snapshot of a relationship with God.

4. By "charge" we mean exhorting the engaged couple (or either person) to fulfill a specific marital, spiritual, or life responsibility. For example, "I charge you, Charles, to be the spiritual leader in your home and to teach your family to be focused on God." Or, "I charge you, Julie, to be not only a wonderful homemaker but also a wonderful lover to your husband for as long as you live."

Printed in the United States
By Bookmasters